Augsburg's
Last
Eagles

Colors, Markings, and Variants of the Messerschmitt Bf 109 from June 1944 to May 1945

Augsburg's Last Eagles

by Brett T. Green
Artwork by Thomas A. Tullis

EagleFiles #3

Color Notes

Color interpretation from black and white photographs amounts to educated guesswork, at the very best. The advent of computer technology has greatly aided in this endeavor. The computer has, through grayscale comparison and analysis, eliminated much guesswork from the evaluation of true colors.

ISBN 0-9660706-5-8

Library of Congress Catalog Number 00-107661

First Edition

Printed in Korea

Library of Eagles

Eagle Editions Ltd.

Post Office Box 580
Hamilton, MT 59840 USA
www.eagle-editions.com

We are interested in hearing from those who may have photographic or data material for use in future publications.

INTRODUCTION

Our understanding of late-war *Luftwaffe* fighter camouflage has changed considerably over the last three decades.

German aircraft that survived World War Two were initially treated at best as war trophies, and more usually as junk. Those aircraft fortunate enough to survive the war were customarily repainted in garish color schemes and markings that bore little resemblance to their original finish.

The majority of these rare surviving aircraft were carelessly left outdoors to deteriorate over time. As often happens with the relics of recent history, very few people considered the intrinsic value of these specimens until almost all of them were scrapped or had rotted away.

Until the 1960s, there was a wide perception that German fighter aircraft were almost exclusively finished in a scheme of Black-Green, Dark Green, and Light Blue. During the following years, a heightened interest in *Luftwaffe* aircraft and a willingness to refer to RLM sources led to many new perceptions about what camouflage colors were really worn by German warplanes. By the late 1970s the standard day-fighter, maritime, and bomber schemes were well documented, color photographs became available, and first-hand research on surviving original airframes vastly improved our picture of *Luftwaffe* camouflage policy and application.

By 1980, when the number of authentic examples of World War Two German warplanes had dwindled to a handful, a series of revelations regarding late-war *Luftwaffe* camouflage came to light. These included the use of a new day-fighter scheme of brown and greens, in addition to the possible use of new lower-surface colors.

The Messerschmitt Bf 109 was built in greater numbers than any other aircraft of World War Two, with the exception of the Soviet Russian Il-2 *Stormovik*. Out of the 30,500 Bf 109s to leave the production lines, *only one* remains in its original finish today. The camouflage, markings, and lineage of this last original Eagle are examined in this book.

Even given the specific focus on the last year of the Messerschmitt Bf 109 in *Luftwaffe* service, this book does not pretend to exhaustively cover all of the developmental issues, variations, color schemes, and markings applied to the Augsburg Eagle during that chaotic period.

Instead, we present background information and descriptions of color schemes in use on the Messerschmitt Bf 109 up to 1945, wartime photos to illustrate typical schemes and some unusual variations, color profiles to bring these schemes to life, scale drawings, and a detailed examination of the oft-misunderstood conformal cowl found on the final variants of the Bf 109.

These elements are combined to generate a concise but colorful summary of the camouflage, markings, and variants of the Messerschmitt Bf 109 from June 1944 to May 1945.

ACKNOWLEDGMENTS

This book started as a simple discussion about the camouflage and markings of Messerschmitt Bf 109 G-6 W.Nr. 163824, based on my research and photographs of the airframe at the Treloar Technology Center of the Australian War Memorial.

Thanks to the enthusiastic contributions of many others, the scope and contents increased considerably during the course of writing and compilation.

It is appropriate to first thank Benjamin Evans of the Australian War Memorial, who, over a period of five years or so, spent many hours patiently at my shoulder as I photographed, color-matched, and documented the Treloar Center's Messerschmitt Bf 109 G-6/U2. Ben's insights into the origins of this aircraft, and his willing feedback on my work-in-progress, made the task far easier than it might otherwise have been.

Charlie Swank has generously opened his wonderful collection of World War Two photographs, that so graphically illustrate the wide variety of color schemes seen on late-war Messerschmitt Bf 109s. I am constantly amazed that new photographs continue to surface over fifty years after the end of hostilities in Europe.

Thanks also are due to Tony Zammit, Carl Hildebrandt, Jerry Crandall, Bob Rinder, Mike Conner, and the Evergreen Educational Facility, for photographs that appear in this book.

Many experts in the field of *Luftwaffe* aircraft, colors, and markings have happily provided comments and suggestions on the text at various stages. Particular thanks go to John Beaman, who added an enormous amount of value by confirming variants and units for many of the subject aircraft in this book. I am very grateful for the counsel of E. Brown Ryle III, David E. Brown, Dave Wadman, Dr. Charles E. Metz, David Lake, and many others. Thanks also to Ken Merrick for his comments on my original discussion paper.

I am delighted to have Tom Tullis' beautiful color profiles and line drawings in this book. We have been talking about this project for almost two years, and I am very pleased that Tom has made such an important contribution to it.

Judy and Jerry Crandall of Eagle Editions Ltd. have been enthusiastic and active participants in the content and format of the book from our first contact. Jerry's expertise and opinions, combined with Judy's daunting organizational skills, have been a wonderful recipe to ensure a quality outcome. As a first-time author, I could not have hoped for a better experience.

And to my long-suffering family, *thank you*. My wife Debra has shouldered the extra burden with the household and with our children, Charlotte and Sebastian, while I was at my keyboard finishing this book.

In conclusion, I encourage anyone with information or photographs that will further enhance our understanding of this chaotic subject to contact me via the publisher, Eagle Editions Ltd., or at my email address: bgreen@bigpond.com.

Brett T. Green

Georges Hall, New South Wales
Australia

Contents

Introduction v
Acknowledgments vi
Messerschmitt Bf 109 Colors 1944-1945 8
RLM Colors–Background .9
The Gray Years 10
Defensive Colors–Browns and Greens 14
Variations 22
Markings 30
Color Profiles 33, 48
RV Bands, Tactical and ID Markings 34-35
Photo Essay Bf 109 G-6 W.Nr. 163824 36
Late-War Bf 109 Variants–1:48 Scale Drawings 49
Messerschmitt Bf 109 G-6/U4/R3, W.Nr. 163824 54
History of W.Nr. 163824 .55
The Treloar Center Bf 109 G-6–General Features . .56
Camouflage and Markings of W.Nr. 163824 58
Primer and Undercoat 58
Lower Fuselage 60
Upper Fuselage 61
Color Table–Colors used on the fuselage of W.Nr. 163824 62
Spinner and Propeller Assembly 64
Wings 65
Tailplane 65
Undercarriage 66
Markings 66
The Streamlined Nose– A Study of Bf 109 G-10 W.Nr. 610937 69
References 76
The Author 79

Messerschmitt Bf 109 Colors 1944-1945

RLM Colors – Background

One of Adolf Hitler's early acts of defiance in the face of the Versailles Treaty was to establish the State Ministry of Aviation. The *Reichsluftfahrtministerium*, or RLM, supervised the operations and administration of Germany's burgeoning military aviation capability from April 1933 onward.

The *Luftwaffe* was formally unveiled in March 1935. The new body was responsible for flying operations, but the RLM remained the administration authority for all other aspects including the selection of aircraft and the standards of production and paint finish.

The RLM issued orders to aircraft manufacturers and paint factories, specifying aircraft finishes. This was not limited to defining colors and camouflage schemes. The RLM meticulously documented surface preparation, application methods, primers, undercoats, drying times, the number of coats, sealing processes, and the level of buffing.

RLM specifications for colors and camouflage schemes were extremely well documented until November 1941. Written instructions and color chips were supplied to all factories producing fighter aircraft to ensure a standard appearance. There was very little variation of the standard camouflage colors except in those cases where experimental schemes were worn by specific units, such as JG 54 during the 1942-43 period in Russia.

In contrast, by 1944 the worsening war situation had led to a partial breakdown of the system. New paint colors were introduced without the benefit of official RLM descriptions or color samples. The standardization of the late-war Brown, Greens, and oft-speculated Gray-Blue, Green-Blue underside colors was therefore difficult if not impossible to attain.

Thus we must largely rely on sometimes contradictory and fragmentary RLM instructions, and monochrome photographs, to determine the colors applied to late-war *Luftwaffe* fighters.

Opposite page: An unidentified Bf 109G in 74/75/76 Grays (center of photo) rests in an aircraft graveyard. Note the standard camouflage demarcation on the port wing, and the saw-tooth pattern on the starboard wing!

The Gray Years

From autumn 1938, German fighter aircraft were finished in a splinter pattern of RLM 70 Black-Green and RLM 71 Dark Green on upper surfaces and fuselage sides, with their lower surfaces painted RLM 65 Light Blue.

This scheme suited the requirement for avoiding detection on the ground in the dense woods of northern Europe. However, the large areas of dark colors were unsuitable for the *Luftwaffe's* aggressive tactics developing throughout 1940. The primary objective of camouflage had shifted from concealment on the ground to concealment of the aircraft in the air.

The RLM's initial response to the changing situation was to order the lower surface camouflage color to be painted higher up the fuselage sides. This order took effect during the winter of 1939-40.

By May 1940, RLM 02 Gray was specified in combination with RLM 71 Dark Green as the new scheme for day fighters. During 1940 some *Luftwaffe* units painted their aircraft in field-mixed Gray paints that were more appropriate for operations over the English Channel. It also is possible that stocks of available French paint were employed during that period.

Two new Gray shades appeared at unit level during early 1941. By the time the Messerschmitt Bf 109 F-2 reached the front lines in March 1941, it was factory finished in the new colors of RLM 74 Gray-Green, 75 Gray-Violet, and 76 Light Blue. Fuselage sides were mottled in RLM 02 Gray, 70 Black-Green, and 74 Gray-Green. This new scheme remained the standard for painting the Messerschmitt Bf 109 on the European Continent until well into 1944.

The Messerschmitt Bf 109 formed the backbone of the *Luftwaffe* fighter arm when German forces commenced "Operation Barbarossa", the invasion of Russian territory in Eastern Europe, on 22 June 1941. As previously noted, the new Gray colors were the official camouflage paints by that time.

However, some units experimented in the field with segmented schemes of Tan, Greens, and White. The extreme conditions during the Russian winter also frequently required the upper surfaces of fighter aircraft to be partially or fully covered with a temporary whitewash.

The Messerschmitt Bf 109 also was deployed in North Africa to support the Afrika Korps. Initial aircraft retained their European Gray color scheme, but soon were repainted in more appropriate shades of Sand and Green on upper surfaces, and a more vibrant Blue for lower surfaces.

Opposite page: A Bf 109 G-6/AS photographed in Reims, France in late autumn 1944. Note the refined cowl, narrow propeller blades, and the short tailwheel. This simply-marked aircraft probably was attached to II./JG 11. The low-contrast color scheme indicates the use of RLM 74/75/76 Grays. The rear fuselage has been oversprayed with an unusual mottle, which probably covers delivery codes and a fuselage band.

"Yellow 12" almost certainly was a Bf 109 G-6 with the tall tail and **Erla Haube** *clear-vision canopy. The rounded bottom to the rudder was a feature of G-6s with tall tails. Camouflage is RLM 74/75/76 Grays. The Black spinner features a White spiral, and the rear sides of the propeller blades are very worn. The wing root fairings appear to be worn back to the bare metal.*

Assuming this photograph was taken in France sometime around September 1944, Bf 109 G-6 "Yellow 12" may have been attached to III./JG 5, in spite of the lack of the III **Gruppe** *bar.*

Three shots of "White 44", a Bf 109 G-6 from an unknown training unit photographed at Lechfeld, Germany in June of 1945. Colors appear to be RLM 74/75/76. The quartered spinner, **Erla Haube** *canopy, wavy camouflage demarcation on the wing leading edges, and the unusual location of the number are noteworthy.*

Defensive Colors – Browns and Greens

The Gray fighter camouflage scheme was ideal when the *Luftwaffe* was conducting an offensive war across the English Channel. The Gray colors provided effective camouflage over the water and against the cloudy skies of northern Europe.

By 1944, however, the *Luftwaffe* was well and truly on the defensive. With overwhelming Allied airpower, acute fuel shortages, and a lack of experienced aircrews, it became critically important to protect the German fighter force on the ground. Improvised blast pens and forests provided a measure of security. Camouflage colors also reflected the shift in the *Luftwaffe*'s fortunes. Brown and Green shades were introduced as a more effective way to conceal aircraft from aerial attack.

The chaotic war situation led to a partial breakdown of color standardization, so that not all changes can be traced to a specific RLM order.

On 1 July 1944 the RLM issued a document (GL/C-10 IV E) containing reference to colors 81, 82, and 83. That document foretold that RLM 81 Brown-Violet and 82 Light Green would be applied to aircraft that otherwise would have worn colors 70 and 71. By mid-1944, the same also applied to bombers, transports, and some training aircraft.

By August 1944 at least two RLM orders noted the withdrawl of RLM 74 Gray-Green. It was to be replaced by RLM 83 Dark Green. The default fighter camouflage scheme therefore was colors 75 Gray-Violet and 83 Dark Green on the upper surfaces, and color 76 Light Blue on the lower surfaces. In practice, however, color 74 Gray-Green frequently was seen in use on aircraft built well after August 1944.

There also is ample evidence that RLM 81 Brown-Violet was used in conjunction with RLM 83 Dark Green as a factory-applied camouflage scheme on the Messerschmitt Bf 109 K-4, and on remanufactured airframes. Furthermore, color 81 often was applied in the field as an additional mottling shade.

RLM 81 seemed to be a particularly unstable shade. The factory-applied color frequently took on the appearance of a rich chocolate Brown. However, color 81 also could appear as a faded Olive Drab shade, a medium Brown (sometimes with a pinkish or a Violet hue), or even a distinct Tan.

Some of these discrepancies may have been the result of field-mixed paints, but variations in application and heavy weathering clearly took their toll of the intended shade.

"White 2", a Bf 109 G-10 with small wheel bulges on the upper wings. The location of the photo is not identified, but likely this was an aircraft of IV./JG 27 in Germany during the spring of 1945. The prominent RV band of JG 27 is a faded shade of RLM 25 Green. The colors appear to be RLM 75 Gray-Violet and RLM 83 Dark Green with a dark overspray on the rear fuselage, which has significantly darkened the appearance of the rear fuselage compared to the fresh RLM 76 Light Blue on the engine cowling. The dirty exhaust stain is typical.The Bf 109 G-14 in the background also is noteworthy, featuring a spotty camouflage scheme in RLM 75/83/76.

This aircraft is a Bf 109 G-10 or G-14/AS attached to NJGr. 11. The camouflage scheme is RLM 75 Gray-Violet and RLM 83 Dark Green on the upper surfaces, with RLM 76 White-Blue on the lower surfaces. There is noticeable contrast between the White of the number "11" and the light color of the fuselage cross. It is possible that the cross had been "toned down" with the lower surface color to minimize contrast in low light. The softer demarcation between the colors on the rear fuselage indicates that the area may have been repainted at some point.

Here is a Hungarian Bf 109 G-10 of Ung.J.St./101, that surrendered with II./JG 52 at Neubiberg in May 1945. At least one other Hungarian Bf 109 G surrendered at the same time. Colors are RLM 75 Gray-Violet and RLM 83 Dark Green, with the lower surfaces in RLM 76 Light Blue. The large number "12" is Red. The aircraft has a Yellow cowl band and rudder, and its fuselage cross is unevenly filled-in with RLM 75. The **Hakenkreuz** *on the tail also has been painted out with the same color. The spinner is quartered in White; the wing root panel is painted Black.*

*"White 43", **werknummer** 463147, also was photographed at Lechfeld. The external trim tabs and pointed bottom corner of the rudder indicate that the aircraft probably is a G-14, as those features were not common on tall-tailed G-6s. The aircraft seems to be finished in a faded and patchy scheme of RLM 75 Gray-Violet and RLM 83 Dark Green. The lack of an aerial mast, the soft-sprayed spinner, the filthy exhaust stain, and the almost complete absence of paint on the propeller blades are of further interest.*

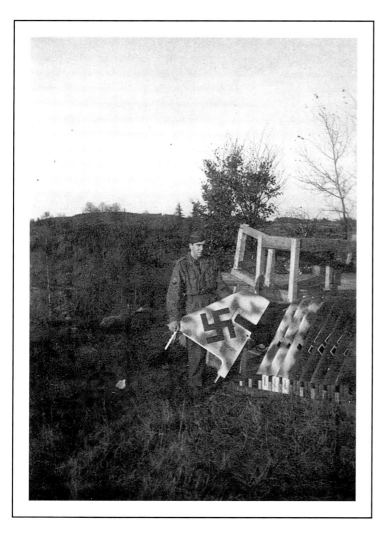

Racks of tall wooden tails for Bf 109s, in a meadow production facility. The two distinct styles of camouflage finish are noteworthy. Pre-painted components such as these tails led to many aircraft wearing hybrid camouflage schemes.

Two close-up views of "Red 4", a Bf 109 G-14. The bulge accomodating the MW-50 tank behind the cockpit is clealy visible in the first photo. Additional details including the canopy restraining wire, cockpit air intake scoop, and folding handholds also are evident. The fuel triangle is an unusual style, indicating the use of C3 100-octane fuel, and probably is Red in color. Upper surface camouflage probably is RLM 81 Brown-Violet and RLM 83 Dark Green, as indicated by the very low contrast between the colors.

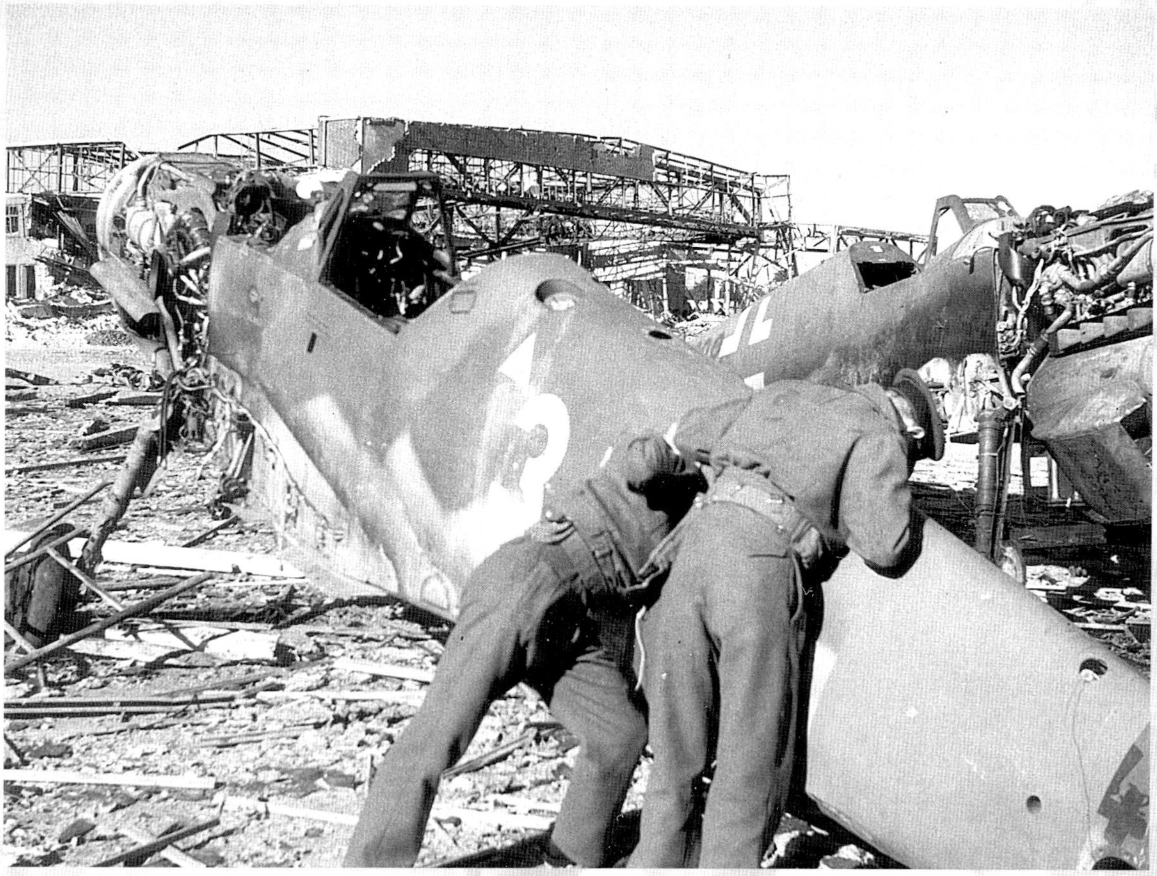

A Bf 109 K-4, "White 3", of I./JG 27. Note the broad Green RV band of JG 27. The last four digits of the werknummer *were sometimes painted on the rear fuselage of late-war Bf 109s. This aircraft appears to have that feature, but the Green RV band now obscures all but the Black "4" digit. This aircraft illustrates one of the standard color schemes seen on this ultimate variant of the Bf 109. Colors are RLM 81 Brown-Violet and RLM 83 Dark Green, with a distinctive "zig-zag" demarcation.*

VARIATIONS

The chaotic war situation inevitably led to a breakdown of RLM color standardization.

Evidence of this breakdown may be seen by the use of primer and marking colors as camouflage, and the widespread appearance of totally undocumented colors on the lower surfaces of fighter aircraft. These colors ranged from Blue-Gray to Yellow-Green. It is not yet known if these colors were standard but undocumented colors, or improvised field and factory mixes.

Special duties also sometimes required special camouflage schemes. Messerschmitt Bf 109s conducting high-altitude fighter escort missions, as well as those operating as night harrassment bombers, wore a scheme of overall RLM 76 Light Blue.

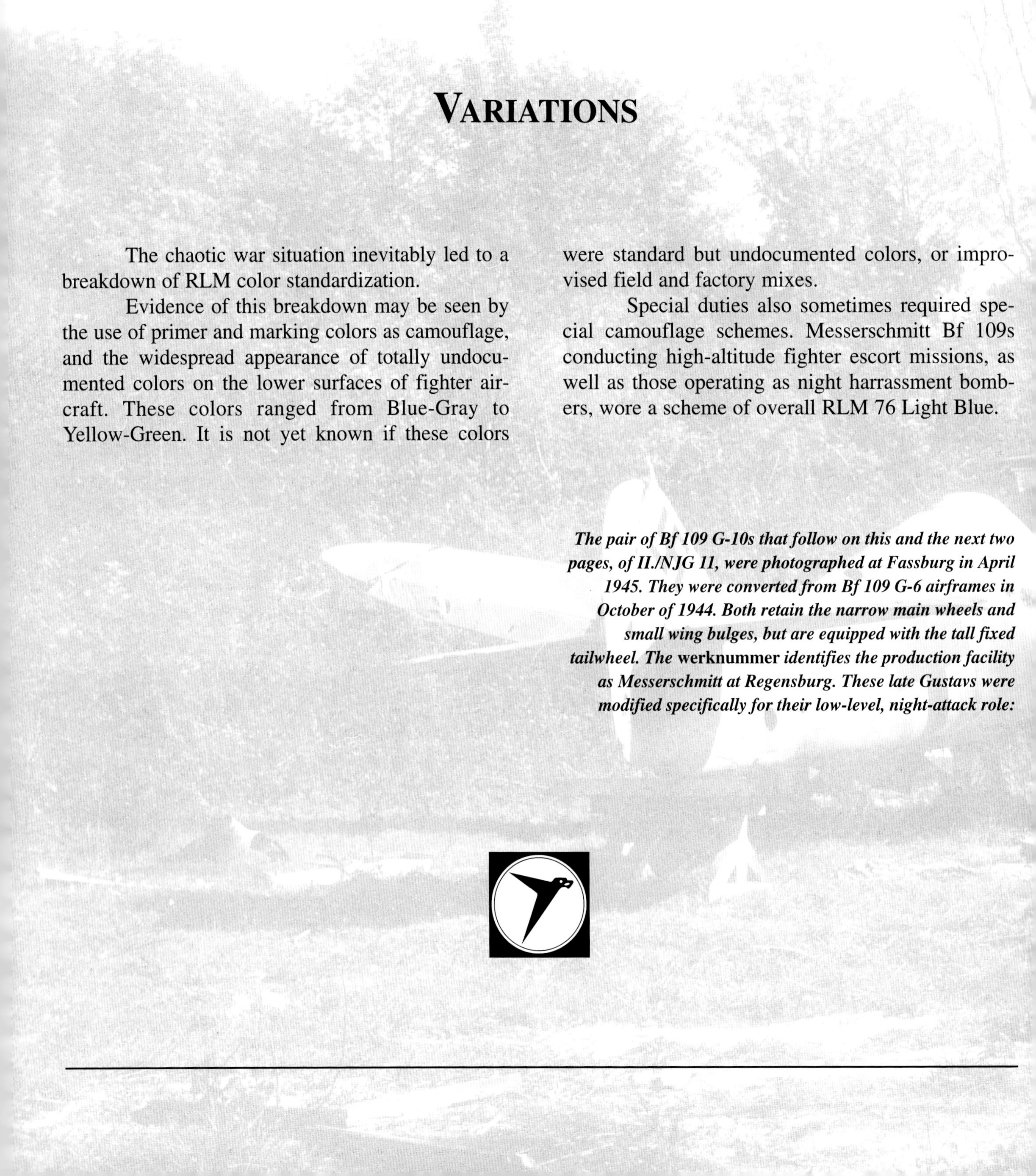

The pair of Bf 109 G-10s that follow on this and the next two pages, of II./NJG 11, were photographed at Fassburg in April 1945. They were converted from Bf 109 G-6 airframes in October of 1944. Both retain the narrow main wheels and small wing bulges, but are equipped with the tall fixed tailwheel. The **werknummer** *identifies the production facility as Messerschmitt at Regensburg. These late Gustavs were modified specifically for their low-level, night-attack role:*

- *The exhaust glare shield was extended further down on both sides, to not only help hide the location of the aircraft but to improve visibility for the pilot.*
- *A small sliding window was added to the port side of the canopy. The Bf 109 was notoriously difficult to maneuver on the ground, and at night visibility must have been very poor indeed. The sliding canopy section may have helped the pilot get his bearings while taxiing, in addition to providing a reflection-free (side) view of a target area or an airfield.*
- *A small, half-moon shaped external mirror was added above the canopy.*
- *A centerline bomb rack would have been fitted. It is not clear from the photographs whether these racks were the ETC50/VIId rack for four 50kg bombs, or the ETC500/IXb rack for carrying a single bomb of up to 500kg.*

The colors of these Bf 109 G-10s are simple in the extreme. Camouflage is limited to overall RLM 76 Light Blue, and markings are White except for the tiny **werknummer**, *the Black and White* **Hakenkreuz**, *and the simplified Black* **Balkenkreuz** *on the lower surfaces of the wings. The Black section of the spinner spiral on "White 44" seems to be partly oversprayed with a lighter color. There are at least three possible reasons for this:*

- *To reduce the contrast between the Black spinner and the White spiral to minimize front-on visibility. If this was the requirement, the color may be RLM 75 Gray-Violet, or RLM 02 Gray.*
- *Increase the visibility of the aircraft front-on to minimize the possibility of "friendly fire" in murky conditions. If this was the intention, the color may be Red or Yellow!*
- *The lighter shade may be due to overspray from when the White spinner spiral was painted.*

Overall RLM 76 Light Blue Bf 109s also were used in other functions and by other units. Bf 109 G/Ks used as high-altitude escorts to protect overloaded Fw 190 A8/R8 **Rammjägers** *from Allied fighters wore the same color scheme. These units included JG 54 and 2./JG 3. Some of the specialized "Mosquito Chasers" of JGr 25, JGr 50, NJGr 10, and NJGr 11 also wore overall RLM 76.*

44

The fascinating series of pictures that follows was taken at Neubiberg after II./JG 52 surrendered to the Allies in an en-mass fly-in on 8 May 1945. In the background is "White 11", a Bf 109 G-10 with the name "Rosemarie" painted in flowing script along the port fuselage. As a Bf 109 G-10 delivered after autumn of 1944, "White 11" should have been wearing upper-surface camouflage of RLM 75 Gray-Violet and RLM 83 Dark Green. However, the aircraft wears an unusual patchy scheme. The basic camouflage colors (on the mid- to rear fuselage) seem very light, perhaps either the result of extreme fading, or perhaps they represent the use of non-standard colors as camouflage. If we assume the center of the fuselage cross is painted according to regulation RLM 83, then the color used for the solid patch between the cross and the aircraft number probably is RLM 75. A lighter color is clearly visible on the fuselage spine and forward of the cockpit, perhaps RLM 77 Light Gray (a color usually reserved for markings and stencils), or a mixed Light Gray. The engine cowl is a darker solid color, consistent with RLM 75. "White 11" also sports a Yellow band around the middle of the engine cowling, a Yellow rudder, a White spiral on its Black spinner, and a short II Gruppe *bar.*

The aircraft in the foreground presents further evidence to support this argument. Werknummer *613168 is a Bf 109 G-10 with very pale upper surface colors. The contrast between the Black of this aircraft's* Hakenkreuz *and its other colors is extreme. It either is an example of heavily-weathered RLM 75/83, or the intentional use of RLM 75 Gray-Violet and a lighter color as camouflage. RLM 76 Light Blue is the most likely color for the lower fuselage, as indicated by the slight contrast with the lighter of the upper surface colors. Sources indicate that this aircraft did not carry a number, rather simply the White II* Gruppe *bar. The rudder is Yellow.*

An unidentified Bf 109 G-6 wearing a very unusual solid upper surface camouflage scheme. The standard factory finish has been replaced by a solid coat of a darker color—possibly RLM 74 Gray-Green or RLM 83 Dark Green. The wing roots of this aircraft have been painted Black. Note that the rear sides of the propeller blades are heavily worn, revealing the shiny metal beneath.

This Messerschmitt is either a Bf 109 G-6 or a G-14. Note the short tail, small wheel bulges on the upper wing, and the long tailwheel strut. The missing canopy was a clear-vision **Erla Haube**. *It could be a G-6 or G-14 of the 782xxx* **werknummer** *series. Some of that batch of aircraft are known to have had tall tailwheels. This aircraft displays some interesting camouflage characteristics. The fuselage seems to carry a pattern typical of remanufactured aircraft. Probably it is finished in RLM 81 Brown-Violet and RLM 83 Dark Green on the spine, and either RLM 76 Light Blue or a Sky shade on the fuselage sides and lower surfaces. The sides carry a sooty Black exhaust stain and a sporadic light mottle. The camouflage on the wings is a simplified, non-standard pattern. The lighter of the two colors may be either RLM 75 Gray-Violet or RLM 81 Brown-Violet. The other color on the starboard wing is noticeably darker than the RLM 83 Dark Green on the spine of the aircraft, and darker even than the dark color on the port wing. This extreme contrast may indicate either a very fresh coat of paint, or a non-standard darker color used on the starboard wing. Possibilities include RLM 70 Black-Green, or even a field mix of Dark Gray.*

Two photographs of "White 16", a Bf 109 K-4 of 9./JG 53 in southern Germany. The Black RV band of JG 53 is clearly visible in the picture. Also of interest is the coloring of the engine cowl, which appears to be a replacement painted RLM 75 Gray-Violet and RLM 83 Dark Green. The remainder of the fuselage is painted in RLM 81 Brown-Violet and RLM 83 Dark Green. A heavy exhaust stain obscures the hard-edged, wavy demarcation line between the upper and lower fuselage colors.

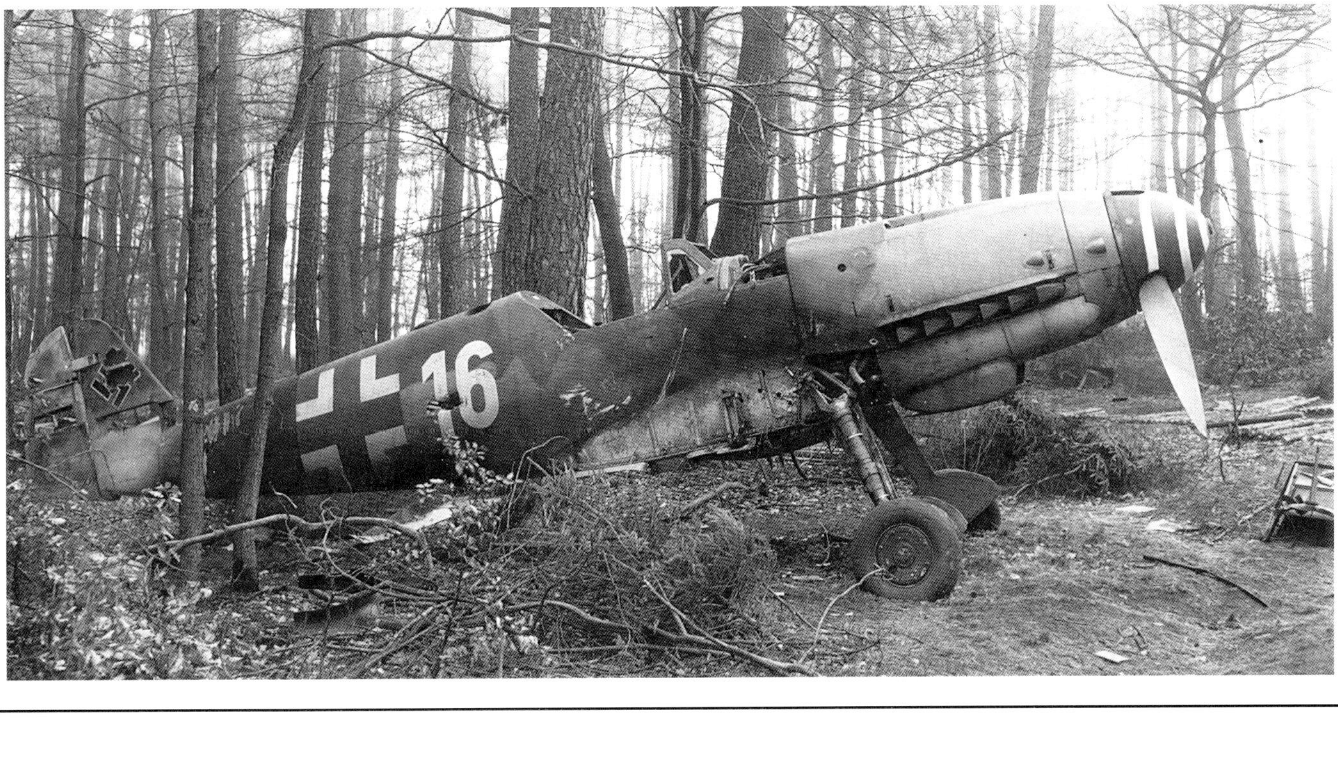

Markings

Late-war Messerschmitt Bf 109s commonly wore special identification markings. Included were color nosebands, color rear fuselage bands, color rudders, and unit-specific RV (*Reichsverteidigung*, or Reich Defense) bands.

Aircraft operating on the southern front of Germany and Hungary frequently were seen with their forward cowls painted Yellow, or with a Yellow band around the cowling. A Yellow chevron, which sometimes was carried over to the top of the wing, was carried on the lower port wing of ground-attack aircraft.

RV bands were colorful bands around the rear fuselage of fighter aircraft, that were designed to assist German flak units, ground troops, and other fighter pilots in identifying friendly aircraft. An order was issued in February 1945 that all fighter aircraft were to wear these colors, formalizing a practice common on the Western Front since mid-1944. Owing to more pressing issues, the order was only sporadically observed.

A listing of the RV bands allocated to units equipped with the Messerschmitt Bf 109, together with color artwork, appears in the Profiles section of this book on pages 34 and 35.

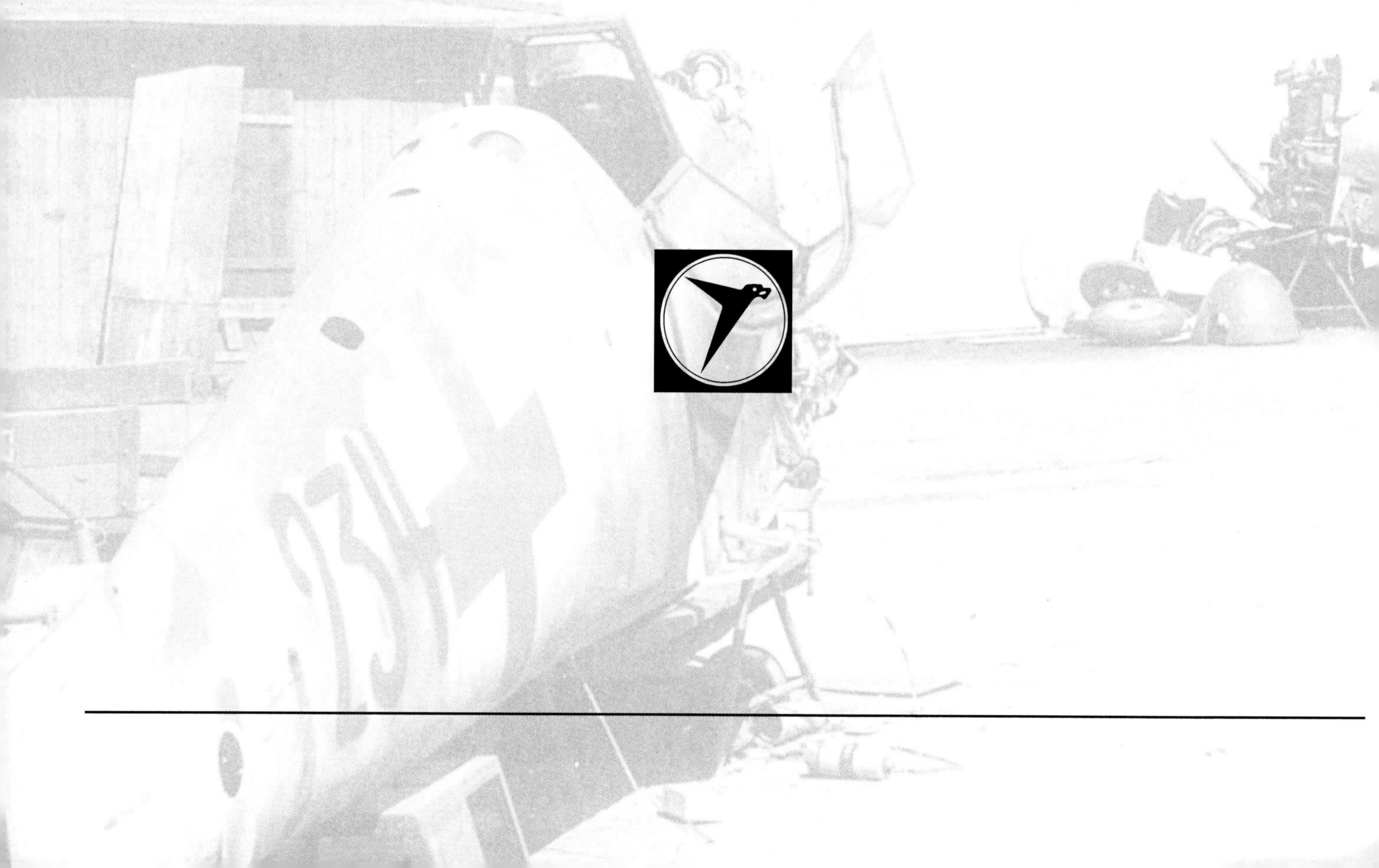

Bf 109 fuselages rest in a compound at Fürth Airfield, near Nuremburg. Fürth was the base of a fighter training unit, JG 104. Three-digit numbers (as seen on Bf 109 G-6 "Yellow 387" in the background) sometimes were seen on late-war fighter training aircraft. The airframe in the foreground bears three roughly spray-painted numbers, used as an expedient identification sometimes seen on late-war BF 109s before they received their unit markings. It represents the last three digits of the aircraft's werknummer. *This airframe is a Bf 109 K-4, possibly having the full* werknummer *334234. An early, framed canopy props up the rear fuselage of this Bf 109 K-4.*

Major Don H. Bochkay, commander of the USAAF 357th Fighter Group, posing alongside a Bf 109 G-10 at Neubiberg during July of 1945. Note the narrow White spinner spiral, and the Yellow band around the nose. The Yellow band was an identifying mark for the southern front.

A Bf 109 G-10 seen at Salzburg, Austria in May 1945. This machine features narrow wheels and the small upper-wing bulges. Clearly shown is the sloppy redesignation sometimes encountered on German fighters toward the end of the war. A large "5" was hastily painted out with a dark color, possibly RLM 70 Black-Green, followed by the overpainting of a Yellow "2" with little regard for the existing camouflage pattern. The high contrast between the upper surface colors suggests a finish of RLM 75 Gray-Violet and RLM 83 Dark Green. The hard-edged, spotty mottle also provides interest.

Bf 109 G-6 “White 3” W.Nr. unknown
(see page 27)

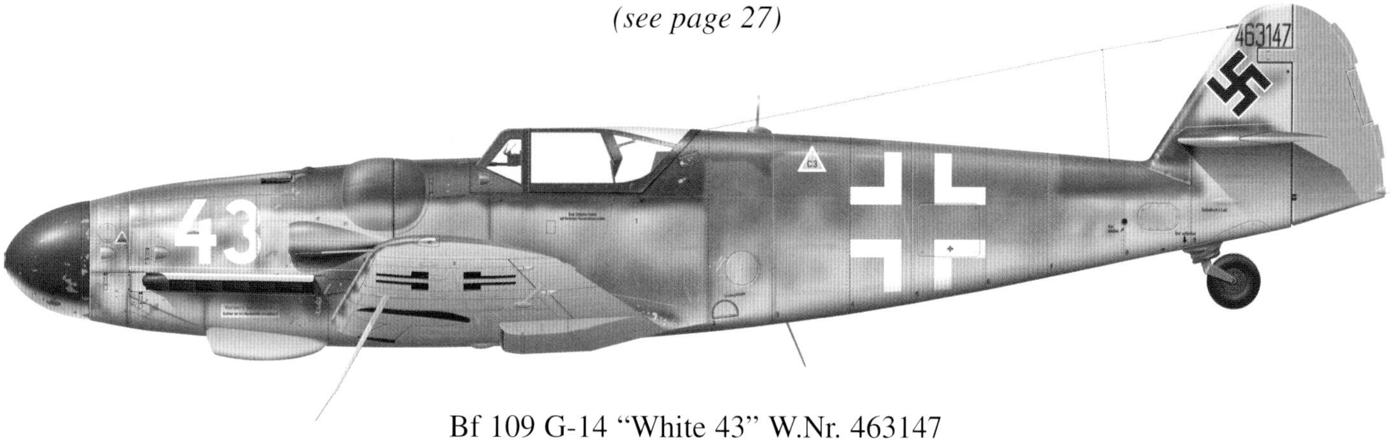

Bf 109 G-14 “White 43” W.Nr. 463147
Lechfeld, Germany June 1945 *(see page 18)*

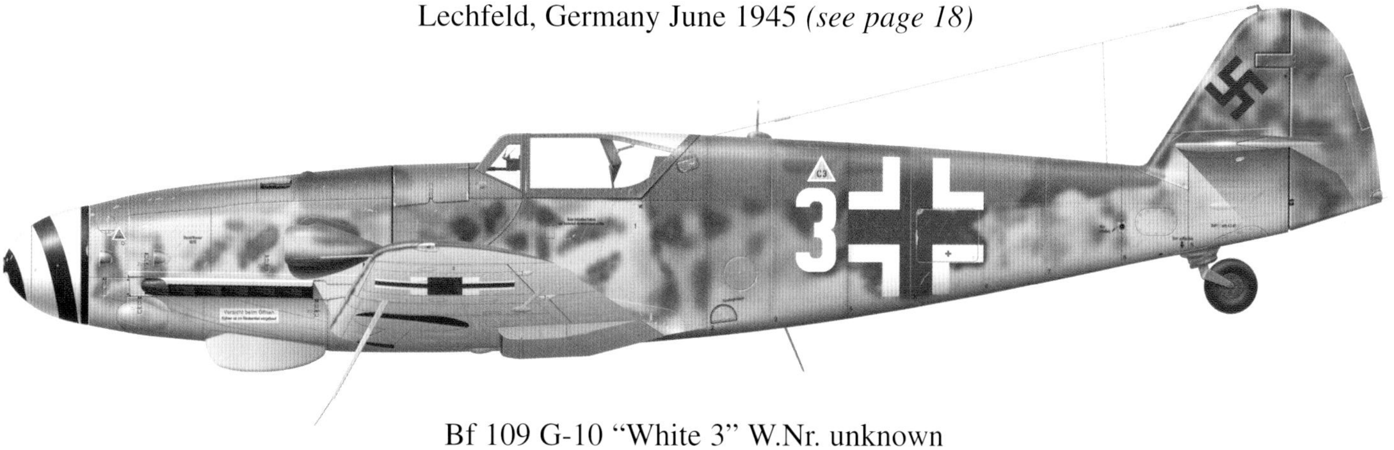

Bf 109 G-10 “White 3” W.Nr. unknown
(see back cover)

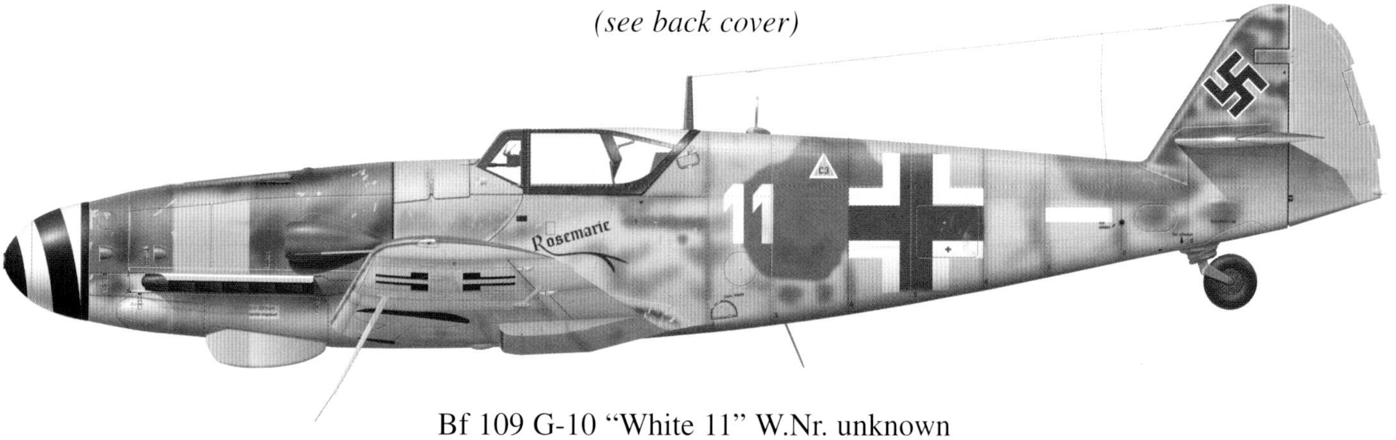

Bf 109 G-10 “White 11” W.Nr. unknown
Neubiberg, Germany May 1945 *(see pages 25-26)*

Bf 109 Reichsverteidigung Bands, Tactical

Tactical Markings

Flight Leader

Mediterranean Theater

Eastern Theater

Reichsverteidigung Bands

KG(J) 6

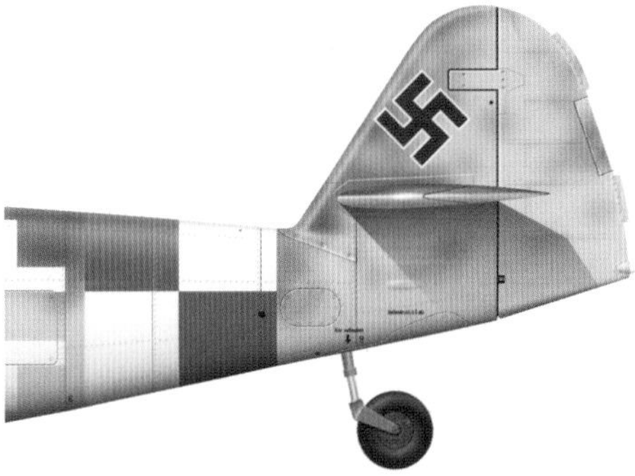

KG(J) 27

JG 1

JG 5

JG 6

JG 11

JG 53

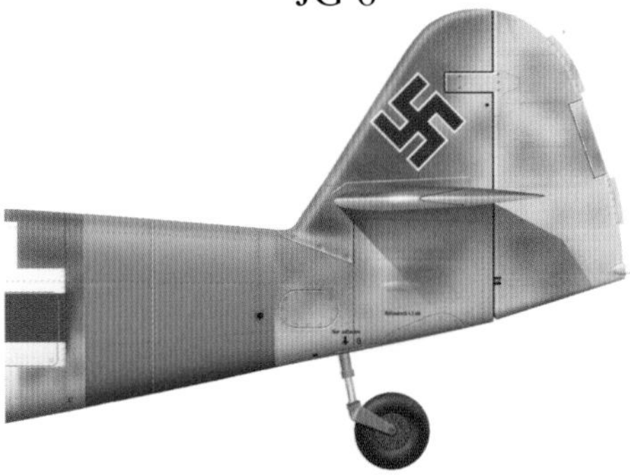

JG 54

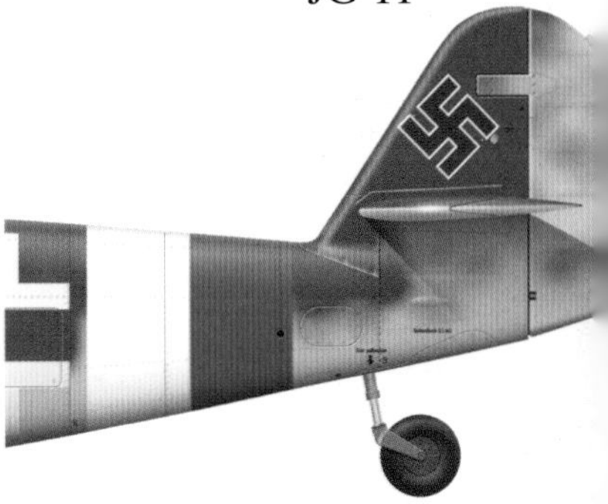

JG 77

and Identification Markings

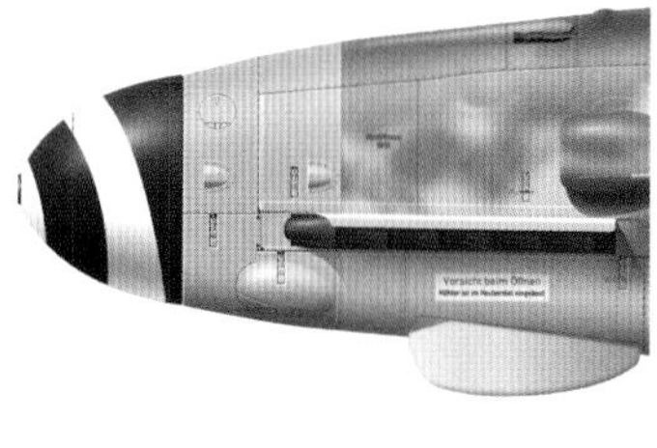

Luftflotte 4

Luftflotte 4

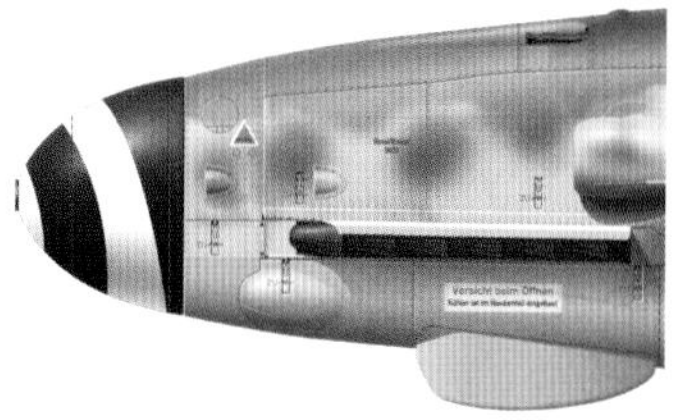

ID Markings

JG 4

JG 2

JG 3

JG 51

JG 26

JG 27

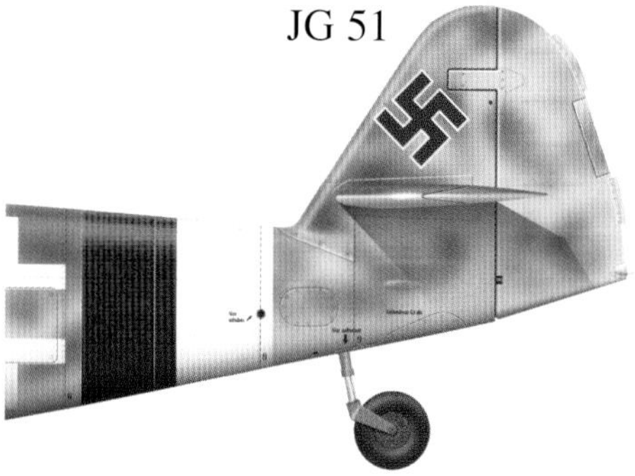

JG 52

JG 300 Early

JG 300 Late

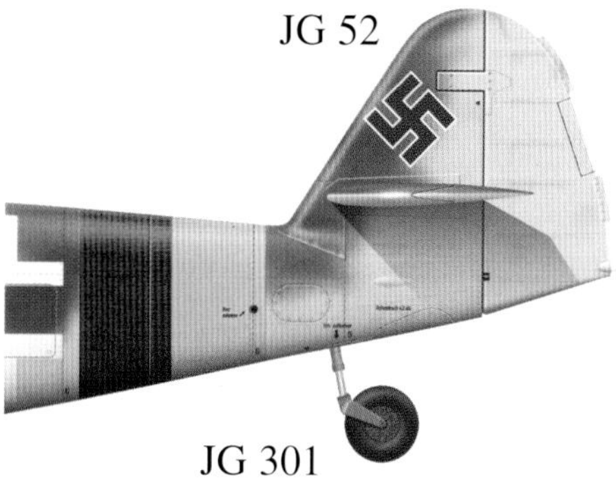

JG 301

PHOTO ESSAY OF MESSERSCHMITT Bf 109 G-6 W.Nr. 163824

(described in detail from page 55)

Starboard fuselage view of Messerschmitt Bf 109 G-6/U4/R3, W.Nr. 163824, at the Treloar Technology Center, Australian War Memorial, Canberra.

The starboard engine cowl is possibly from a Bf 109 G-5, as suggested by the scoop, cover, extra bulge, and small vent. These features provided accomodation and access for the cockpit pressurization gear. Despite this cowl design, the pressurization gear is not installed in either the engine bay or the cockpit.

Patches of primer are exposed in places. At least two different primer colors were used. Spots of Red primer are visible on the raised rivets along the port side of the fuselage and on the canopy. Fabric "pinking" has been used at some stage to cover the flare chute just underneath the starboard windscreen. Red primer was applied to the pinking, although the fabric itself has blown off.

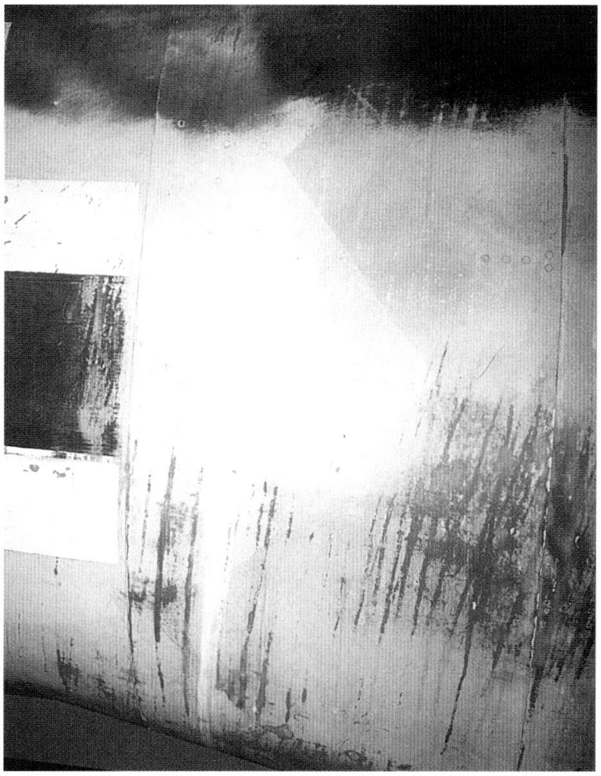

A noticeably different color is applied behind a sharp, ragged masked line along the rear starboard fuselage station 4. This demarcation continues as a jagged horizontal line to the back of the fusealge, isolating the color to a large patch on the rear starboard fuselage side only. This is a lighter, brighter shade that appears as a distinct Yellow-Green color (see page 63.) In contrast to the light, patchy application of the Green-Gray color, this brighter Yellow-Green color displays solid paint coverage.

The lower cowl is painted RLM 76 Light Blue. This color looks significantly "cleaner" and lighter than the mixed Gray color. Light Blue has been applied as a line of soft mottled spots on the upper engine cowl. Curiously, this color also is present on the rear, lower half of each MG cowl bulge. A large portion of Dark Green has worn off the fuselage breech cover (immediately in front of the cockpit), revealing the Light Blue undercoat.

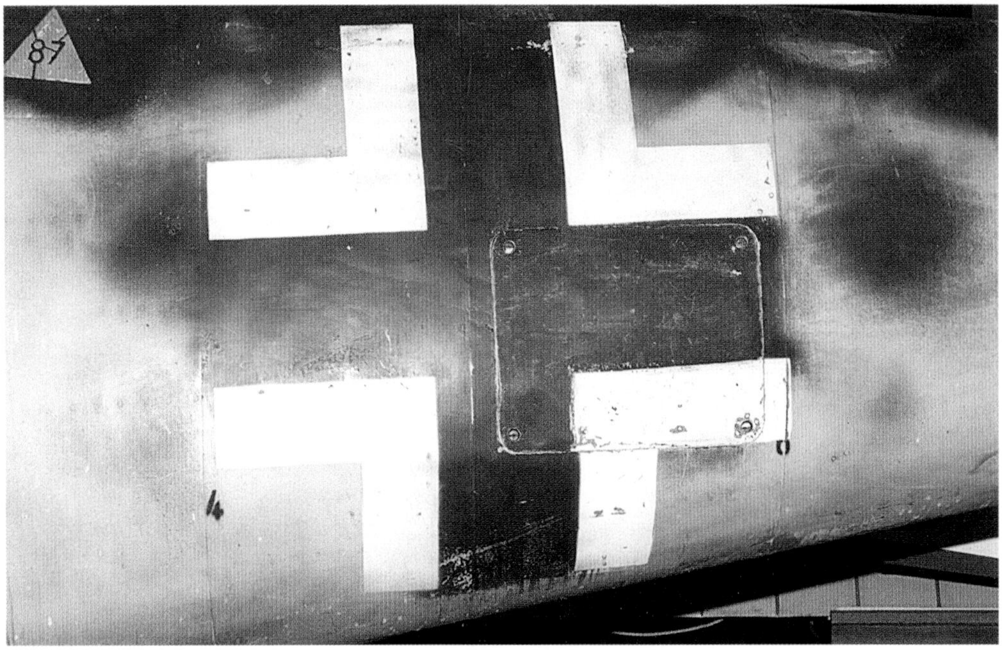

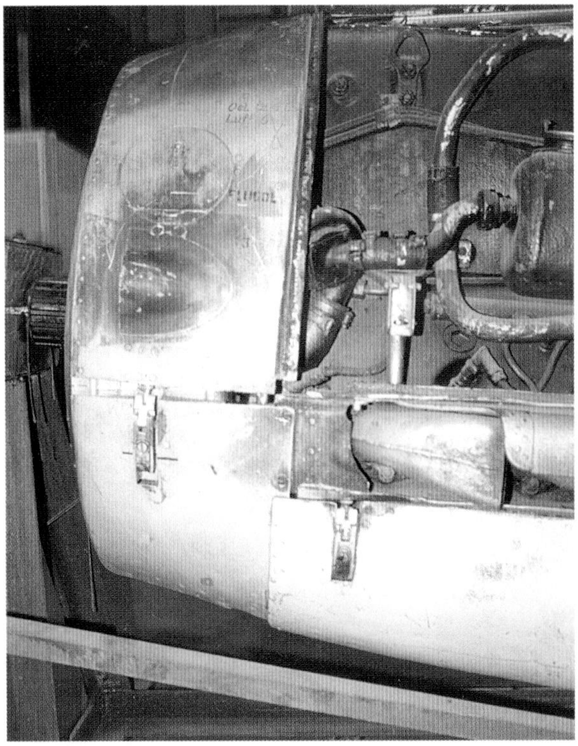

This close-up view of the port forward cowl area shows the hand-painted oil-filler instructions and cowl latch details.

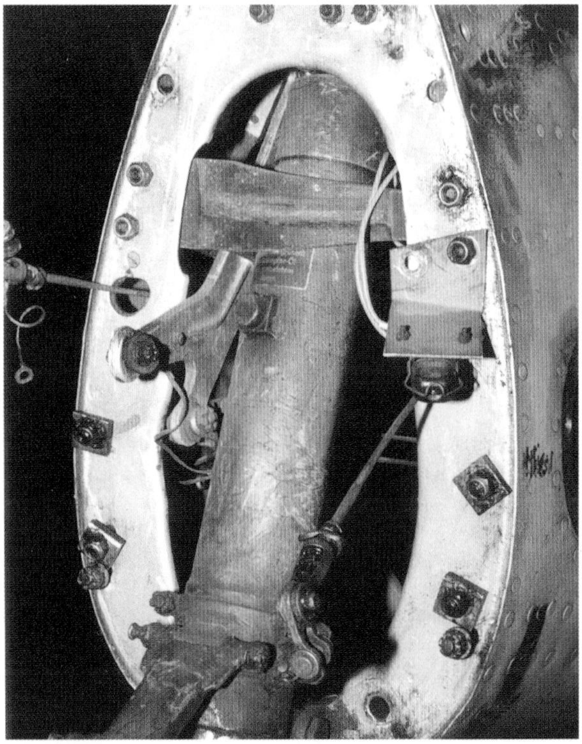

Tail wheel strut and fuselage station detail view. The strut is painted RLM 02 Gray. Note the data plate above the red-tipped grease nipple. The fuselage station bulkhead remains in excellent condition despite its unpainted state.

Opposite page, top: The starboard **Balkenkreuz** *was painted before the new camouflage colors, as evidenced by a gap between the cross and the new camouflage colors, between which can be seen either the old color or the base coat. The Dark Green center has been masked, but the paint was applied by brush. The cross has been extensively chipped, showing bare metal underneath.*

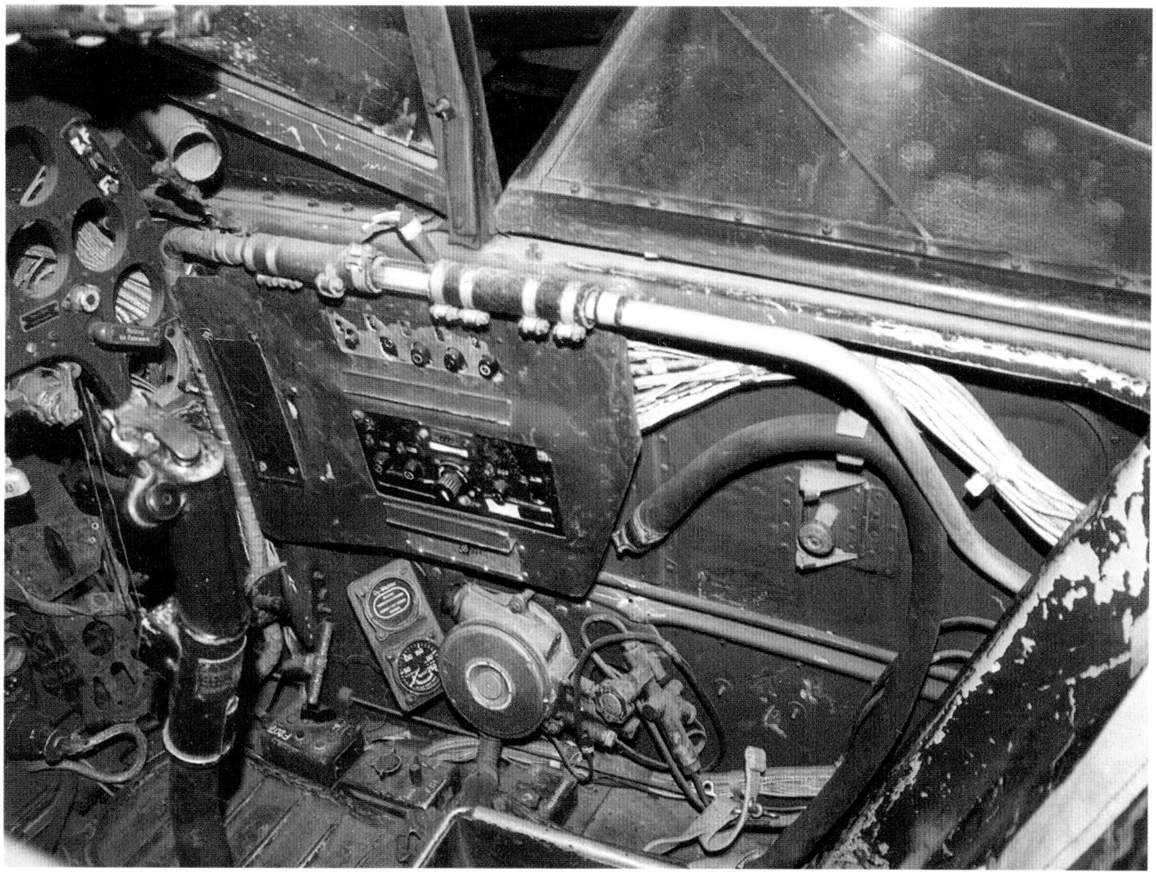

Detail view of starboard cockpit interior. Although most of the panel instruments are missing, as illustrated here the rest of the cockpit is quite complete, to the starboard side radio panel at center of photograph, control stick at left, switches and buttons, and piping and wiring for various systems.

Detail view of starboard lower cowl area, showing prominent center weld seam on the exhaust stacks and RLM 76 Light Blue painted on lower cowl.

Starboard cowl showing features typical of the Bf 109 G-5. The extreme contrast between the RLM 76 Light Blue lower cowl and the Green-Gray fuselage is evident in this and the photograph above.

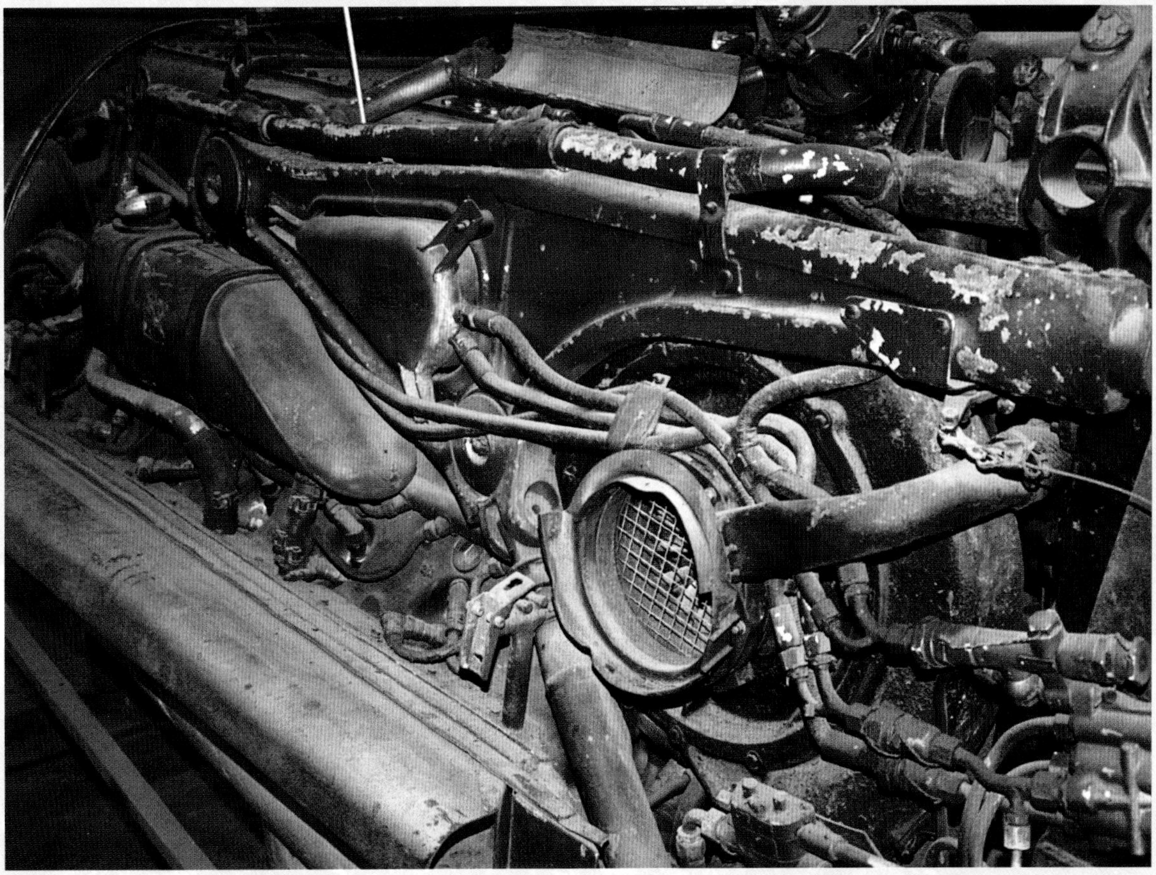

The DB605A powerplant of Bf 109 G-6, W.Nr. 163824. The Red color on some of the engine components is not original; rather, it is a protective coating applied before the aircraft was shipped from Europe to Australia at war's end.

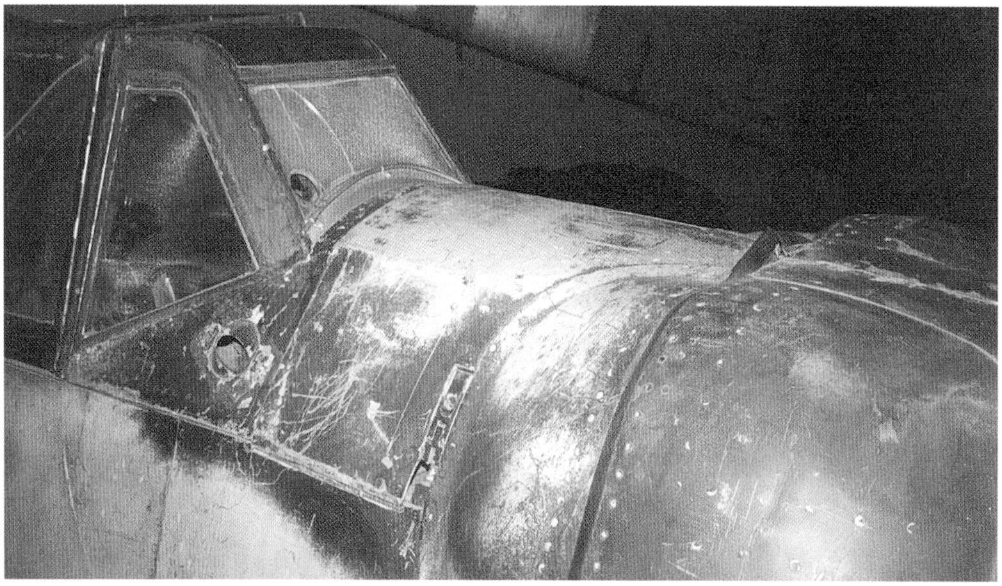

Heavy scuffing to the paint of the gun breech cover, present in photographs taken of this machine at Eggebek in 1945, reveals the RLM 77 undercoat. Note hole in the armored windscreen for a dessicant capsule.

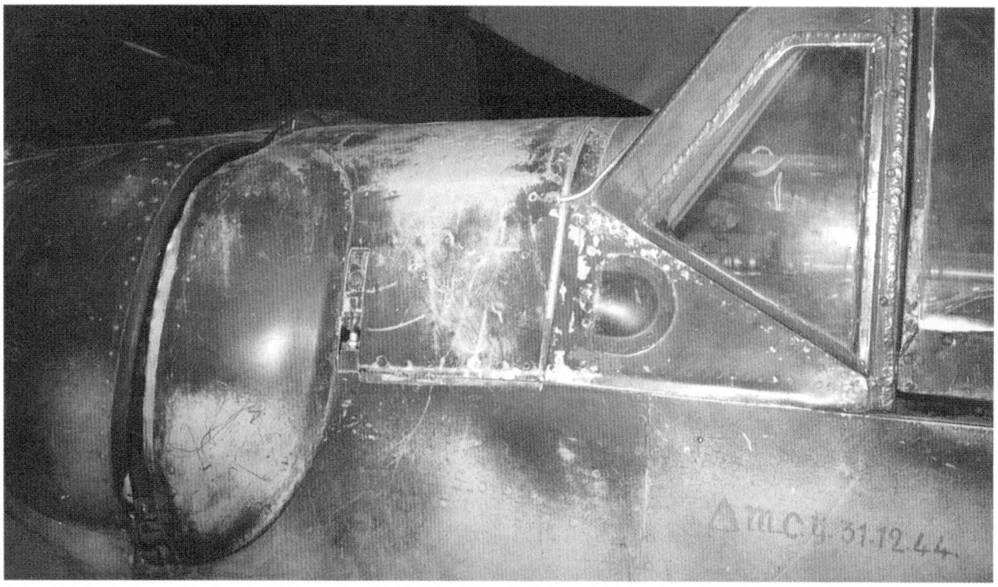

Port upper engine cowl shows patches of RLM 76 Light Blue mottle, or perhaps more likely RLM 77 under scuffed surface of gun bulge. Note the small cockpit ventilation scoop, and date of remanufacture crudely painted in Yellow under cockpit.

Close-up port side view showing details of **Erla Haube** *canopy. Note* **Galland Panzer** *armored glass panel behind the pilot's seat, and Red dive-angle indicator on side of canopy glass.*

Looking aft along starboard fuselage. Note streaky, patchy lower surface camouflage paint colors, filler hatch markings, details of **Balkenkreuz,** *and overall original condition of aircraft.*

Close-up view of cockpit interior, showing panel with most instruments missing, myriad wires, control stick at center with gun trigger.

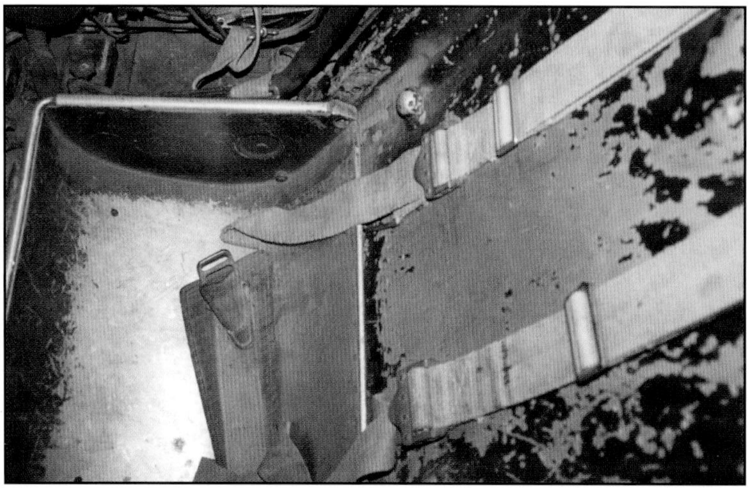

Typical Bf 109 bucket seat. Note the absence of a backrest, and the pale-color harness.

Note how the demarcation between the Green-Gray and Yellow-Green colors continues in a jagged line through bottom of the **Balkenkreuz.**

This close-up view of the upper-right arm of the starboard **Balkenkreuz** *shows details of the hand-applied brush marks, as well as the RLM 02 Gray primer (over panel joins) and bare metal underneath.*

This underside view clearly shows the differences between the RLM 76 Light Blue lower wing area and the "sky" color of the lower fuselage.

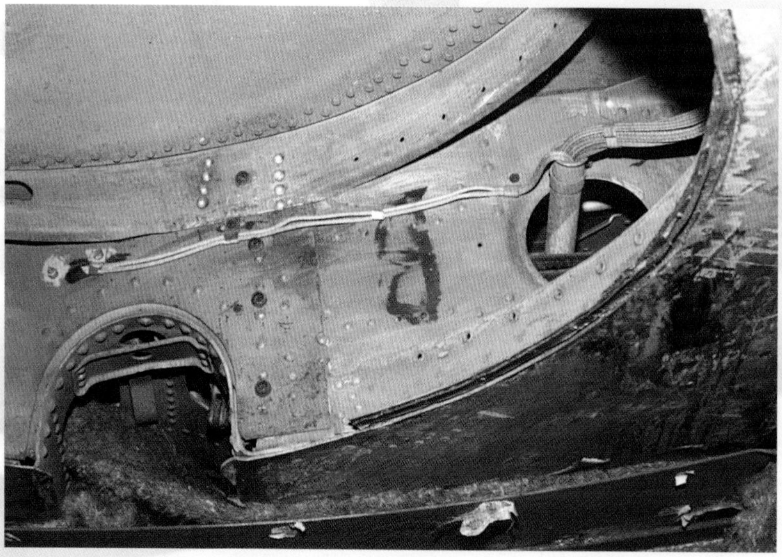

Both wheel wells appear to be painted either RLM 02 Gray, or the mixed Green-Gray color, a rather unusual feature on late-war Bf 109s. The top of the port side wheel well is painted RLM 76 Light Blue.

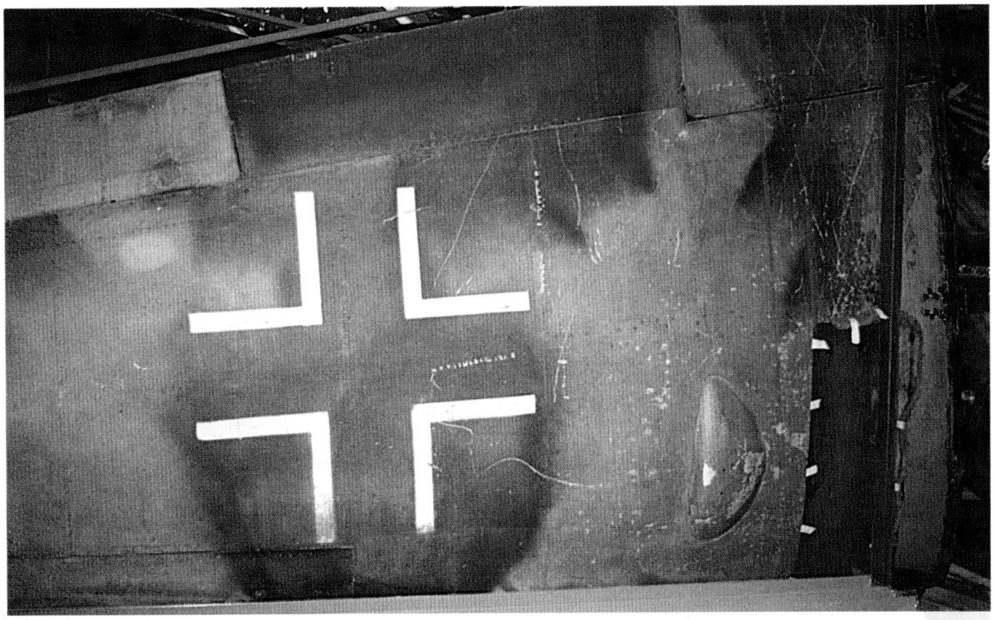

The wings of Bf 109 G-6U4/R3, W.Nr. 163824, have the small, early-style bulges for the narrow wheels. Upper surface colors are RLM 75 Gray-Violet and RLM 83 Dark Green, divided in a non-standard pattern having a soft-edge "saw-tooth" demarcation in places. The RLM 75 Gray-Violet appears to be a fresh coat over existing finish. The starboard aileron has been lightly oversprayed with RLM color 75, with evidence of a repair clearly visible under the thin coat of Gray.

The lower surface of the port wing is painted the mixed Green-Gray color. The aileron has a very thin coat of the mixed Green-Gray, and RLM 76 Light Blue can clearly be seen in large patches on the aileron. The Silver color on the wing, mass-balance, and flap is the residue of a protective skin applied during a failed export attempt that took place around 1979.

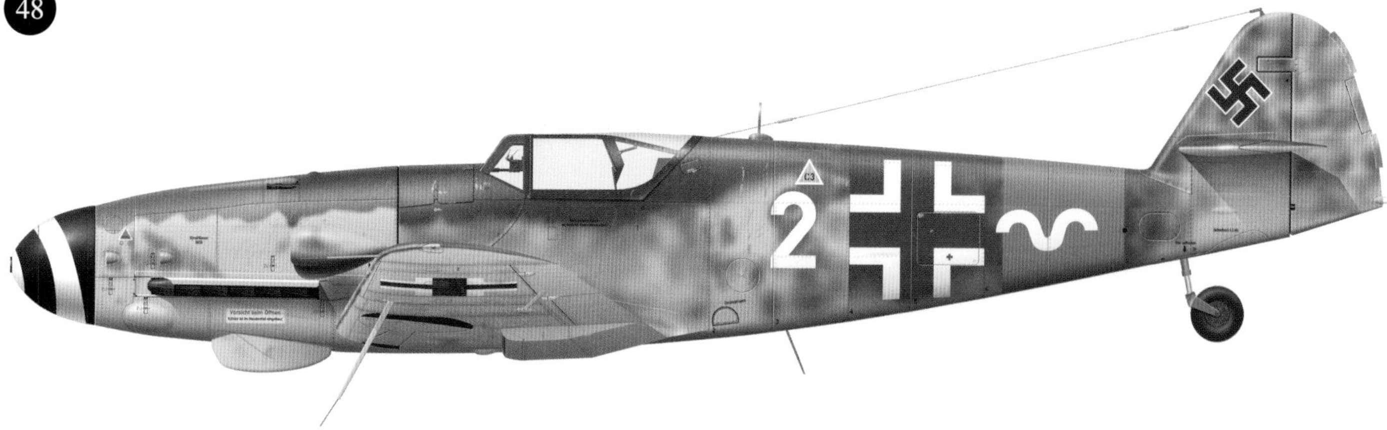

Bf 109 G-10 “White 2” W.Nr. unknown
(see page 15)

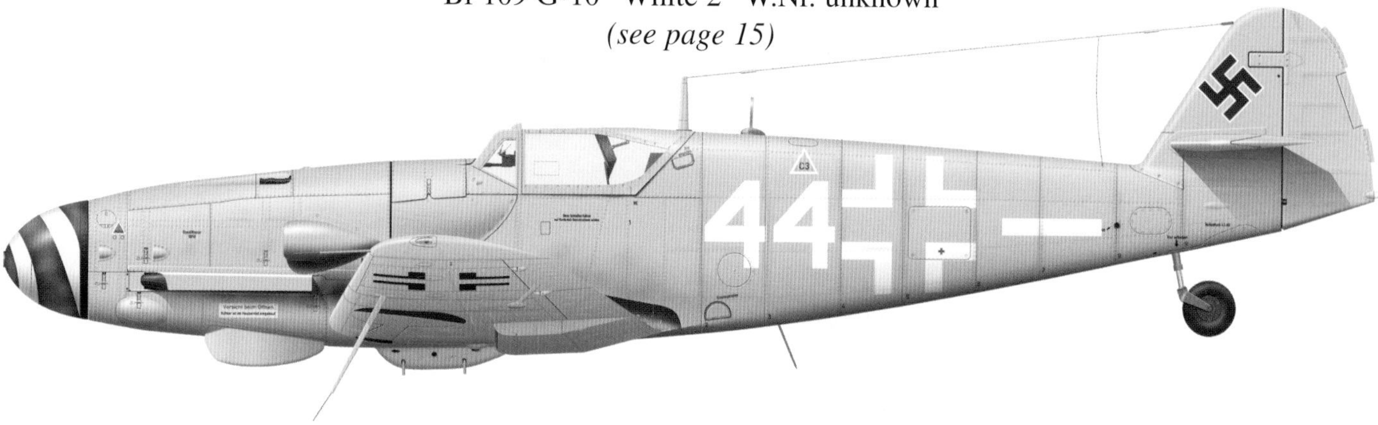

Bf 109 G-10 “White 44” W.Nr. unknown
II./NJG.11 Fassberg, Germany April 1945 *(see page 24)*

Bf 109 K-4 “White 16” W.Nr. unknown
JG 53 *(see page 29)*

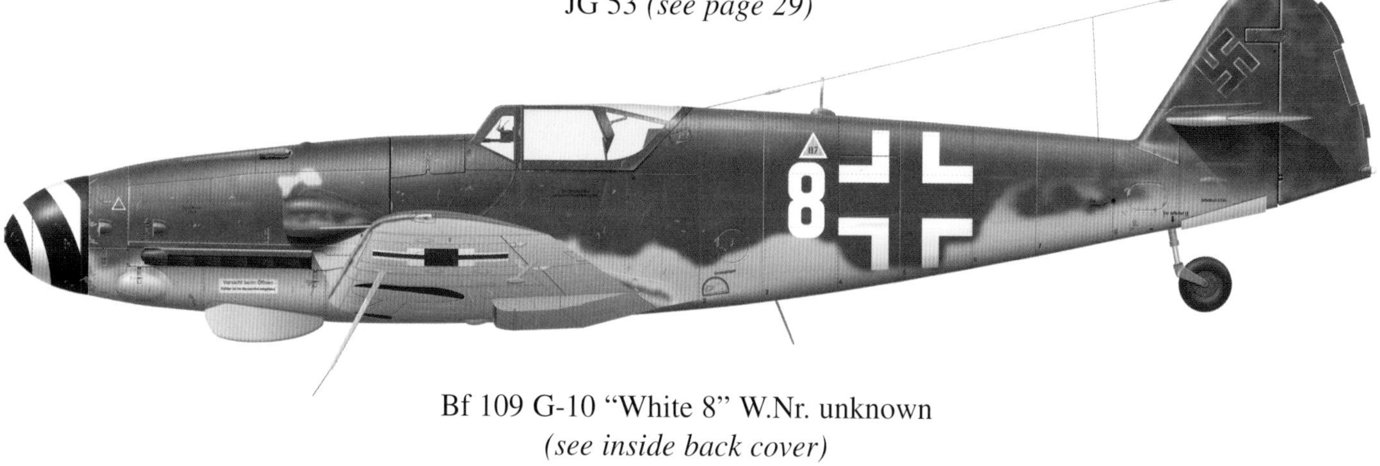

Bf 109 G-10 “White 8” W.Nr. unknown
(see inside back cover)

SCALE 1:48

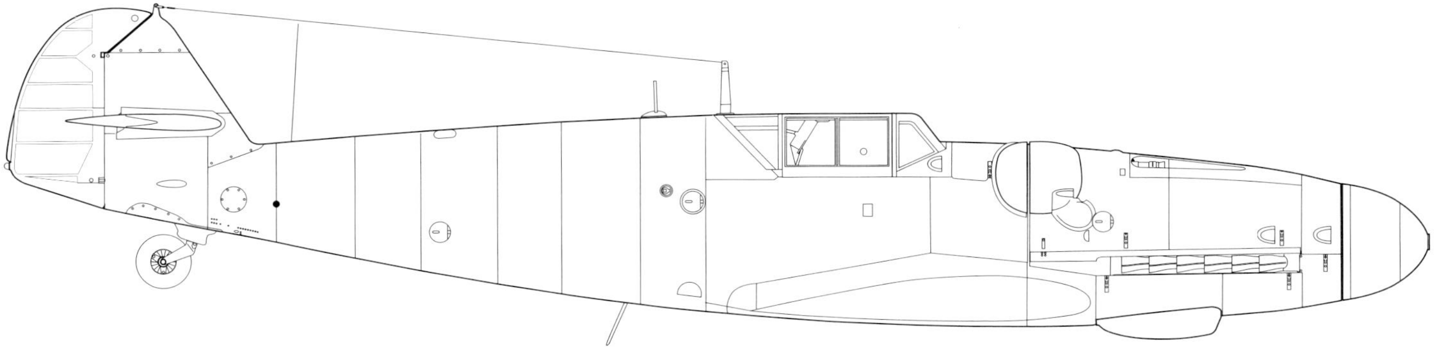

G-6

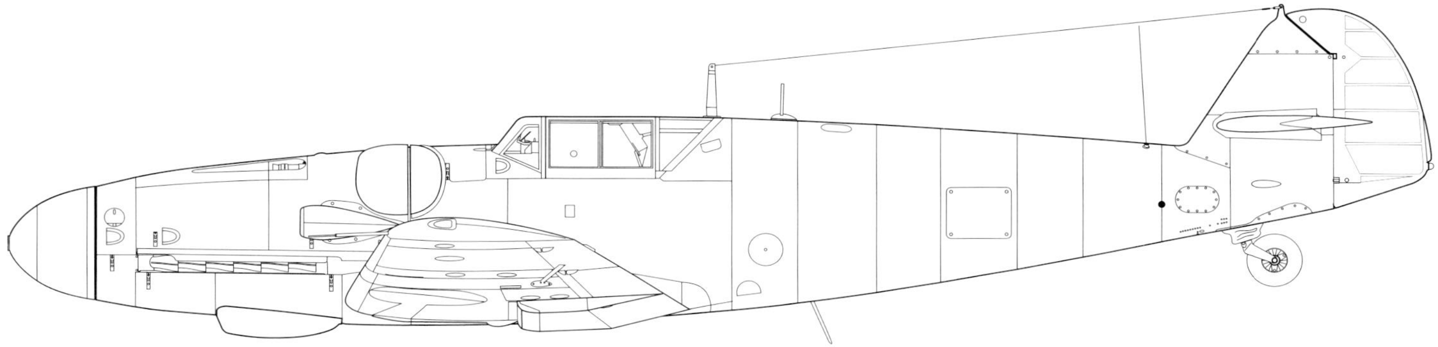

Messerschmitt Bf 109 Series

SCALE 1:48

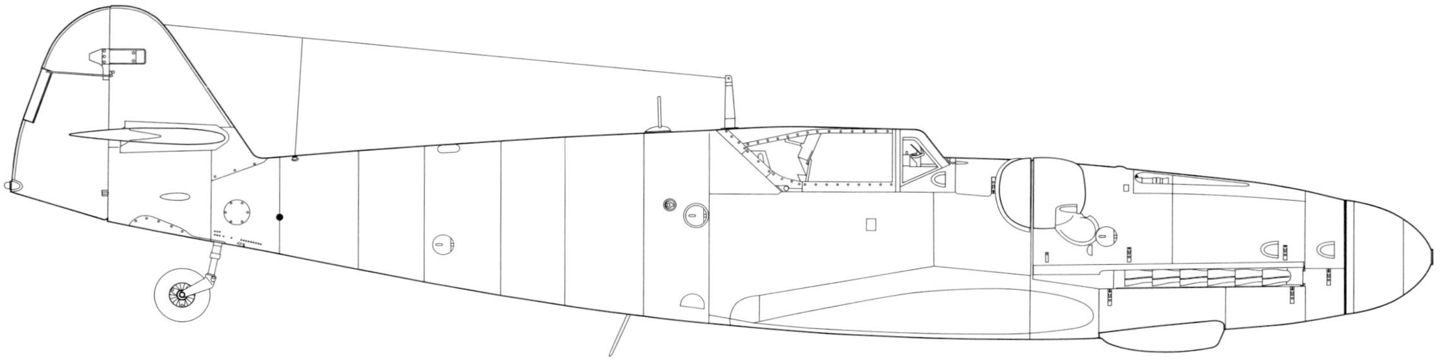

G-14

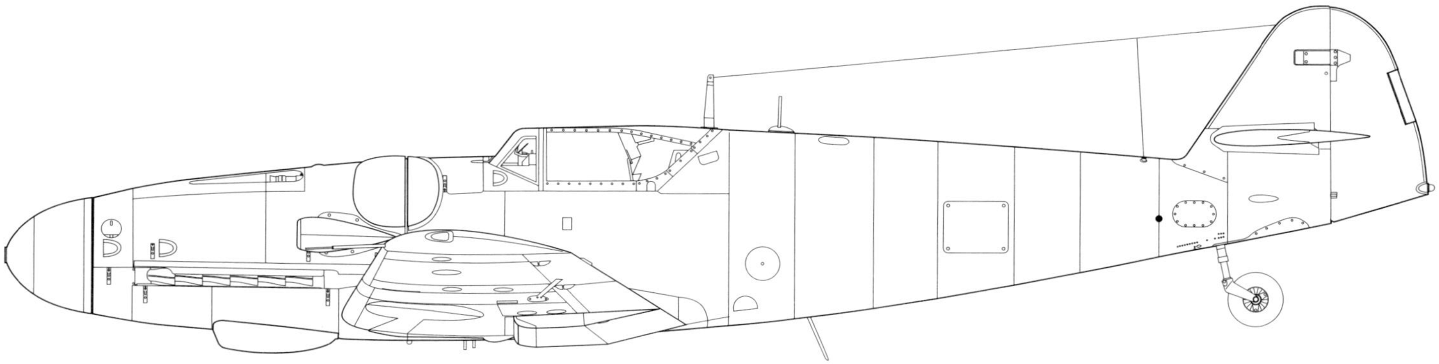

Messerschmitt Bf 109 Series

SCALE 1:48

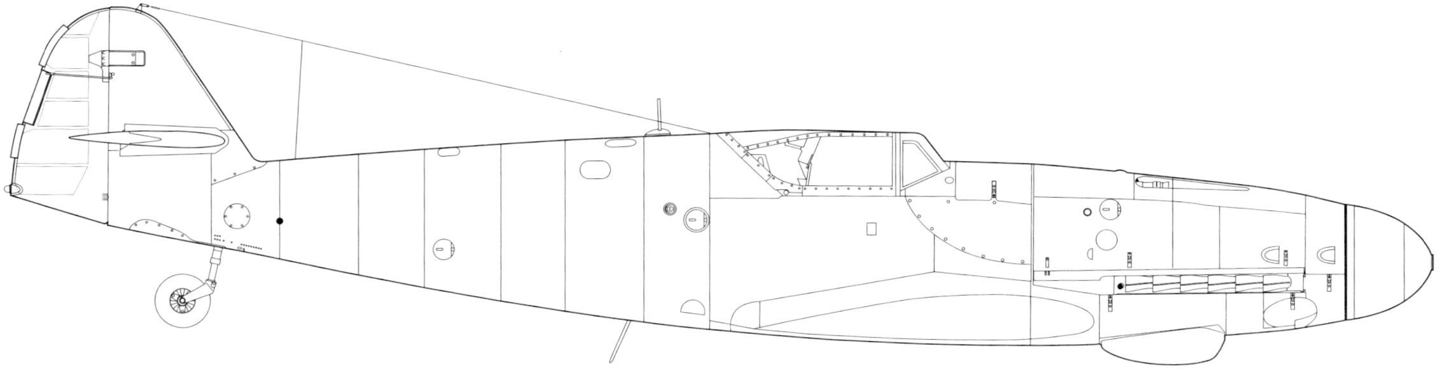

G-10 Type 100

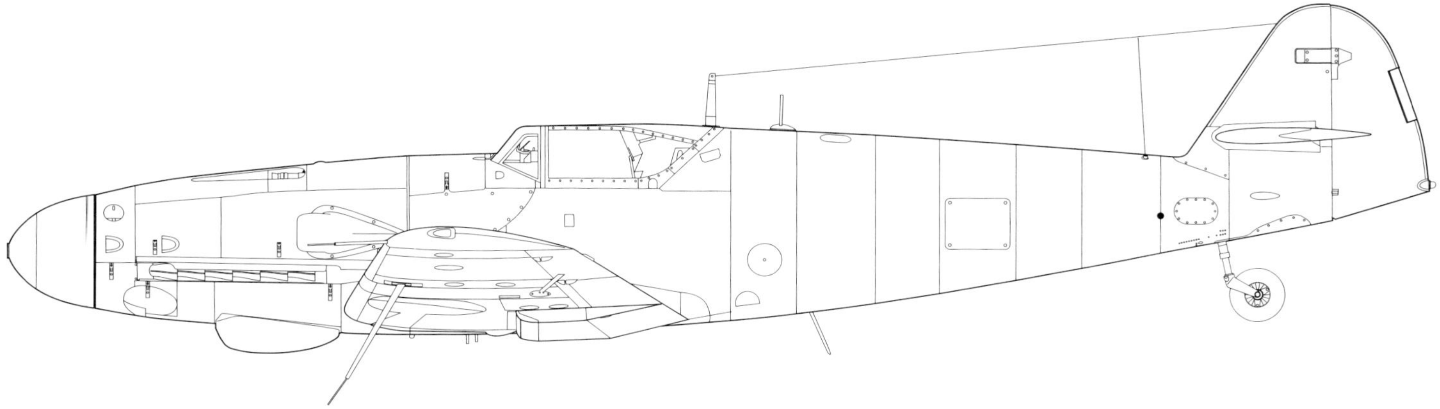

Messerschmitt Bf 109 Series

SCALE 1:48

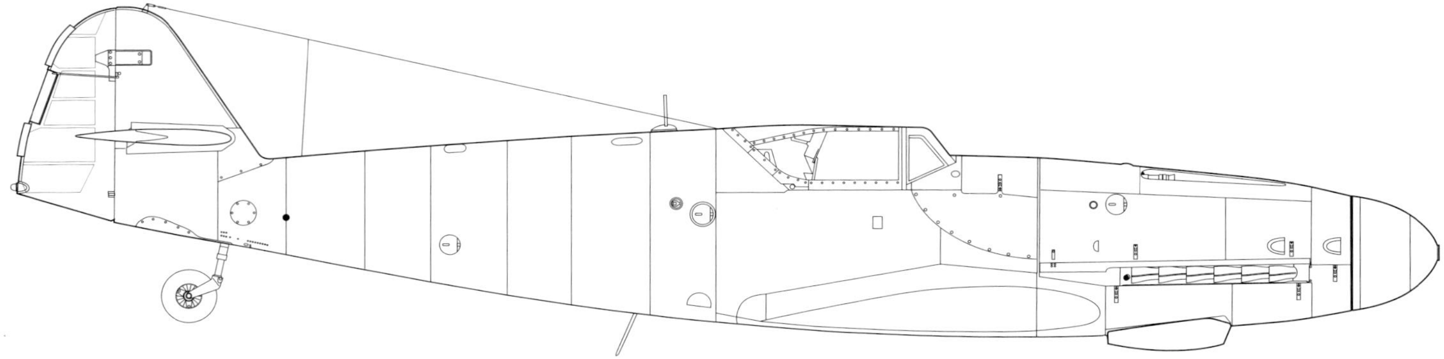

G-10 Type 110

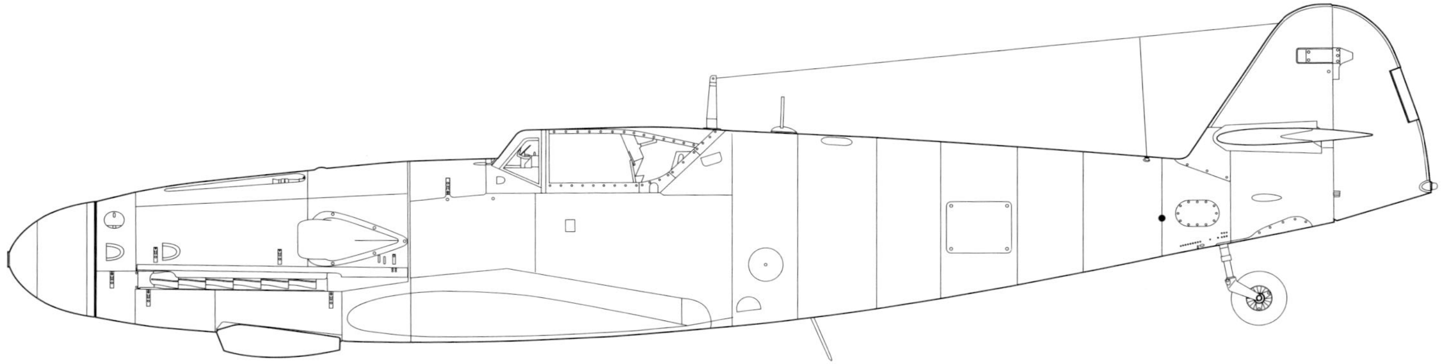

Messerschmitt Bf 109 Series

SCALE 1:48

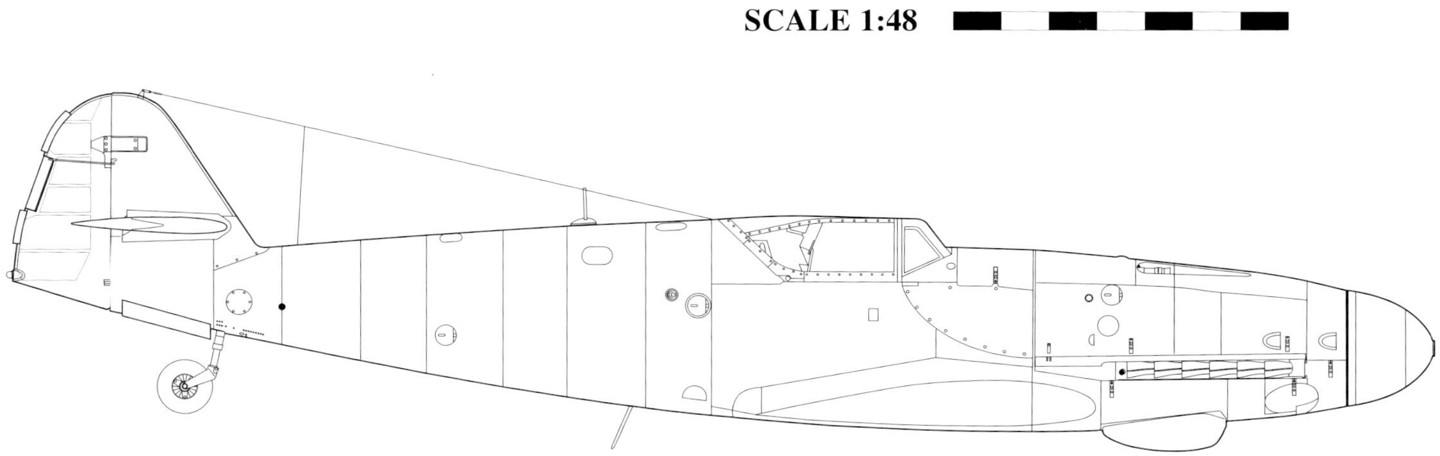

K-4

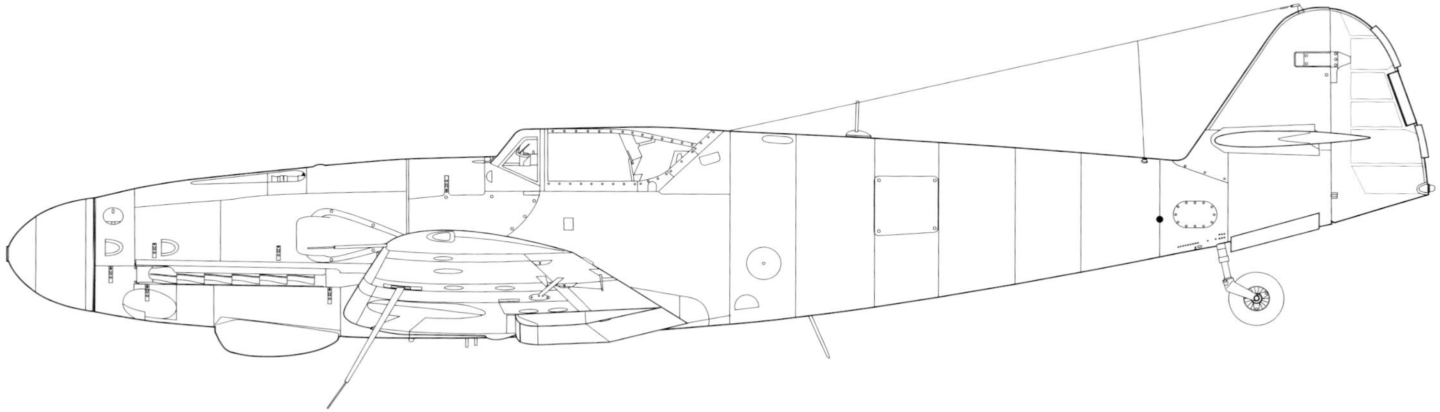

Messerschmitt Bf 109 Series

Messerschmitt Bf 109
W.Nr. 163824

G-6/U4/R3

History of W.Nr. 163824

Due to a remarkable set of circumstances, Messerschmitt Bf 109 G-6 W.Nr. 163824 managed to escape "restoration" and has spent most of the last half-century safely stored.

The aircraft was claimed as a war prize by Allied forces, and shipped from Eggebek airfield in Germany on 4 September 1945. It was eventually delivered to Australia via the United Kingdom.

W.Nr. 163824 was sold to a British buyer in 1979, but the Australian Customs Service blocked its export and confiscated the aircraft. W.Nr. 163824 is currently located, partly disassembled, at the Treloar Technology Center of the Australian War Memorial in Canberra.

W.Nr. 163824 is probably the last remaining Bf 109 in its almost original condition. It still wears its wartime camouflage and markings, and has survived the last five decades remarkably well. Despite its partial disassembly, the Australian War Memorial has all components except some cockpit instruments.

The Treloar Center Bf 109 G-6 – General Features

Werknummer 163824 was an uncommon Messerschmitt Bf 109 G-6, which wore an equally uncommon camouflage scheme (see color photo, page 36).

Although factory production of the Bf 109G-6 ceased in the summer of 1944, this Bf 109 was rebuilt in December 1944 after a hybrid history. The *werknummer* indicates its original manufacture as a Bf 109 G-6 during autumn 1943 by Messerschmitt at Regensburg. At that time the aircraft would have been fitted with the standard, three-section framed canopy, with the *Galland Panzer* armored glass behind the pilot's head.

Probably the most unusual feature of this Bf 109 G-6 is clear evidence that the rear section of the conformal "bulge" associated with the DB605D and DB605AS engines has been removed from both sides of the fuselage. This indicates that, despite its G-6 identity, the fuselage saw service as a different version of the Bf 109 at one time. This mystery is explained by the late-war requirement for the *Luftwaffe* to make full use of all available components.

Around February or March of 1944, this standard Bf 109 G-6 was rebuilt as a G-6/AS, with the more powerful DB605/AS engine that required the installation of a new nose and fairing panels on the fuselage sides below the forward canopy. The aircraft saw service with JG 1 or JG 11 in this configuration until it was damaged in May 1944. After repair, the unlucky machine was once again damaged on a ferry flight before the end of 1944.

The three-letter code and date "MCY 31-12-44" tells us that the aircraft was rebuilt as a standard Bf 109 G-6 by Ludwig Hasen & Co., Flugzeug-Repararatur-Werk, Münster, in December 1944. In this final guise it featured a MK 108 30mm cannon firing coaxially through the spinner (to U4 specifications), and provision for a fuselage-mounted 300-liter drop tank (to R3 specifications—a *Rüststätze*, or field modification).

Werknummer 163824 was captured in its final form before it could be assigned to a new fighter unit. This explains the absence of tactical markings.

There is a prominent, but non-standard, bulge riveted to the top of the port engine cowl just behind the port machine gun trough. This bulge is noticeably larger than the standard round pressed protrusion (on top of the gun interrupter housing) usually seen in this position on a Bf 109 G-6.

Another significant feature is not fully explained by this airframe's hybrid heritage. There is a prominent, but non-standard, bulge riveted to the top of the port engine cowl just behind the port machine gun trough. This bulge is noticeably larger than the standard round pressed protrusion (on top of the gun interrupter housing), usually seen in this position on a Bf 109 G-6.

The starboard engine cowl is possibly from a Bf 109 G-5, as suggested by the scoop, cover, extra bulge, and small vent. These features provided accommodation and access for the cockpit pressurization gear. Despite this cowl design, the pressurization gear is not installed in either the engine bay or the cockpit of W.Nr. 163824.

The style of pressed gun trough insert also is consistent with a Bf 109 G-5 engine cowl. This cowling design was originally intended for use by Bf 109 G variants equipped with cockpit pressurization. Although this included the Bf 109 G-5, further pressurized variants were projected but never built. Therefore it also is possible that this cowl was surplus to the requirement for one of these abandoned projects, and was originally fitted to W.Nr. 163824.

The lower cowl may have been sourced from any type of G-5, G-6, or G-14. It has the smaller radiator housing and no "bumps" on the front, so it certainly is *not* from a G-10 or a K-4.

The aircraft features the *Erla Haube* clear-vision canopy with *Galland Panzer* armored glass, and a Red dive-angle indicator painted on both sides of the canopy side glass. This suggests that the aircraft was intended for use as a fighter/bomber, or (more likely) that the canopy was sourced from a Bf 109 *Jabo*. The armored glass windscreen has a hole on the starboard side for a desiccant capsule, which was used for dehumidifying the windscreen.

A small, triangular werknummer plate is located aft of fuselage station 8 on the starboard side. The *werknummer* is from a batch assigned to Bf 109 G-6s built by Messerschmitt at Regensberg. Not surprisingly, there has been some confusion identifying the sub-type of this aircraft. Some sources claim it is a G-14, others state that it is a G-6/U2. However, despite its somewhat bizarre hybrid elements, the general layout, weapons, powerplant, and *werknummer* all point inevitably to this aircraft being a Bf 109 G-6/U4/R3.

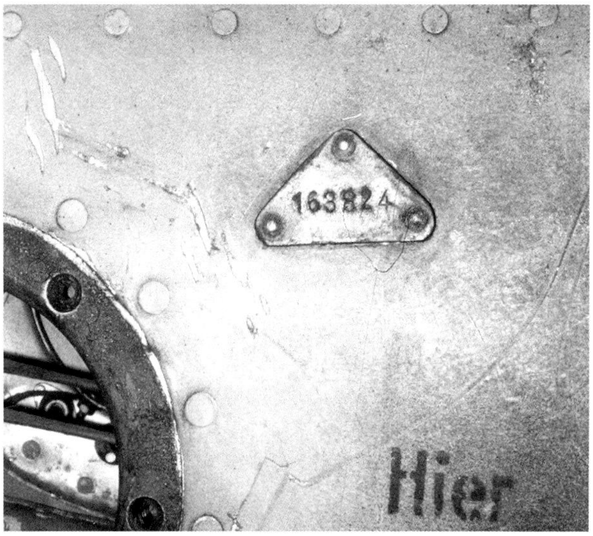

Triangular W.Nr. plate on aft fuselage.

The Treloar Center has no plans to "restore" this aircraft. Their mission is to preserve this significant specimen in its current condition. This policy provides the researcher with a unique insight into the problems of interpreting the application of late-war *Luftwaffe* camouflage schemes.

Camouflage and Markings of W.Nr. 163824

It is now over fifty years since the last Messerschmitt Bf 109 aircraft was painted. We are indeed fortunate to have the opportunity to examine such an original late-war scheme first-hand.

It is important to point out that the aircraft was examined under artificial light, and that fifty years will have had *some* effect on the tone and shade of the original camouflage colors. Therefore, the following interpretation the aircraft's colors should be considered as a reasonable and balanced evaluation rather than a concrete statement of fact. What cannot be denied, however, is that the camouflage finish of this aircraft is well preserved, and exhibits many interesting traits.

The accompanying images are not entirely helpful in displaying the colors of the aircraft, due to a combination of lighting factors and the multiple processes between the time the film was exposed at the Treloar Center and production of this publication.

The color information in the Color Table should be considered more reliable. This Table has been produced using the results of a number of visits to the Treloar Center to inspect the aircraft. An FS-595B color-chip fan was used to compare the colors on the aircraft to Federal Standard colors. Following these initial comparisons, further analysis was undertaken by comparing the colors on W.Nr. 163824 directly to some well-respected sources, including Eagle Editions' *Luftwaffe Color Chart* and *The Official Monogram Guide to Painting German Aircraft 1935-1945* (see References).

The camouflage finish of Bf 109 G-6 W.Nr. 163824 is just as remarkable as its hybrid heritage. The aircraft has been dismantled into separate fuselage, wing, and tailplane assemblies. Wings and tailplane have been stored and are unavailable for examination, but the fuselage is accessible.

The Color Table supplies a description of the camouflage and markings, with Federal Standard color equivalents noted. Although the conclusions are undoubtedly subjective, nevertheless this aircraft may be our best opportunity to understand late-war *Luftwaffe* fighter camouflage schemes more than fifty years after the event.

Primer and Undercoat

Patches of primer are exposed in places. At least two different primer colors were used. Spots of Red primer are visible on raised rivets on the port side of the fuselage and on the canopy. Fabric "pinking" has been used at some stage to cover the flare chute just underneath the starboard side of the windscreen. Red primer has been applied to seal this pinking, although the fabric itself has blown off (see color photo, page 37).

Notwithstanding the presence of this Red primer, large sections of RLM 02 Gray primer also can be found under thinly-sprayed mixed Green/Gray, particularly on the mid-starboard fuselage. Hand-painted RLM 02 Gray primer has been used in a more economical way on the rear of the starboard fuselage, where it is applied only along panel and rivet lines.

The airframe probably received at least a partial base coat of RLM 76 Light Blue before its new camouflage colors were applied. This coat shows through in several places where the dark upper surface colors have been scuffed and worn. It is difficult

Bf 109 G-6 **werknummer** *163824, photographed at Bankstown during the late 1960s.*

to positively establish that the same base coat color of RLM 76 was used on the entire airframe. RLM 77 Light Gray may have been used on the fuselage spine and other parts of the airframe. It also is likely that the camouflage on the starboard mid-fuselage was applied directly over the old camouflage pattern, as a mottle of RLM 71 Dark Green seems to be showing through the new lower fuselage color.

Lower Fuselage

The fuselage sides and undersurfaces are sprayed in a thin coat of a non-standard Green-Gray color. The effect of this color is quite similar to RAF Sky Type "S". The RLM 76 base coat shows through in several patches, particularly on the starboard fuselage. Streaked vertical lines on the starboard fuselage sides point to the Green-Gray color possibly "running" while it was still wet; however, it is equally likely that these streaks are the result of some spilled fluid while the airframe was in storage.

A noticeably different color is applied behind a sharp, ragged masked line on the rear starboard fuselage aft of fuselage station 4. This demarcation continues as a jagged horizontal line to the back of the fuselage, isolating the color to a large patch on the rear starboard fuselage side only. This is a lighter, brighter shade that appears to be a distinct Yellow-Green color (see page 63). In contrast to the light, patchy application of the Green-Gray color, this brighter Yellow-Green color displays solid paint coverage (see color photo, page 37).

Both of these lower fuselage colors are probably what some 1980s sources described as RLM 84, or "sky" colors. This designation was never applied by the RLM, and the colors were probably obtained as a result of mixing stocks of existing paint. It is possible that the colors on the fuselage of W.Nr. 163824 and other late-war fighters may have represented the use of new standard (but undocumented) colors. However, it is more likely that they are a mix of current and/or redundant stocks of 02/76, 76/04, 04/80/21, 65/02/21, 77/76, 77/02, or any number of other combinations.

A number of sources claim that these late-war "sky" colors did not exist, instead contending that the color variation was due to fading or oxidization of standard RLM 76 Light Blue. One argument made to support this premise is that when the "oxidized" layer is removed there is evidence of RLM 76 underneath, proving that the top layer is nothing more than the effect of weathering. However, that argument does not take into account that a thinly-applied layer of a "sky" color over RLM 76 will yield the same result.

There is abundant additional evidence that these colors really did officially exist. Some of the supporting points include the following:

- The "sky" colors appear only on a limited range of aircraft types. These include the late-war Bf 109 G/Ks and Fw 190 Ds. RLM 76 was used widely from 1941, but the "sky-shaded discoloration" is exclusively reported on these late-war types.

- One also might expect that fading or oxidization would apply to more than one color on an aircraft. It could even be argued that darker colors should fade more quickly than lighter colors. However, there are a number of examples of aircraft (including W.Nr. 163824, and color photographs of Fw 190 D-9 W.Nr. 500570) where all the other colors are very close to RLM standards except the "sky" shades. There are streaks on the fuselage of W.Nr. 163824 which look very much like paint runs from the thinly-applied "Sky" shade.

Finally, it is interesting to note that the Yellow-Green shade on the rear of the starboard fuselage is almost an exact match for the color-chip described as "Green-Blue" on page 41 of *The Official Monogram Painting Guide to German Aircraft* (see References). Despite its designation in the Monogram book, the color has been labeled "Yellow-Green" in this document as, *in the opinion of the author*, this name more closely describes the appearance of the color, both on the aircraft and the paint chip.

Upper Fuselage

Upper surface camouflage comprises RLM 81 Brown-Violet and RLM 83 Dark Green. The demarcation is an irregular, scalloped line fairly high on the rear fuselage side, dropping slightly to follow the line of the canopy. This scalloped demarcation continues from the lower front of the canopy to the nose of the aircraft. These upper surface fuselage colors have been spray-painted without the aid of masks, as indicated by significant overspray.

RLM 81 Brown-Violet is applied lightly, with the base coat showing though in several places on the fuselage spine. A soft, spotty mottle of Brown-Violet also is applied to the side of the fuselage. The RLM 83 Dark Green color is heavily applied, with heavy spots of the color applied mainly to the rear fuselage and the engine cowling.

The lower cowl is painted RLM 76 Light Blue. This color looks significantly "cleaner" and lighter than the mixed Gray color. Light Blue has been applied as a line of soft mottled spots on the upper engine cowl. Curiously, this color also is present on the rear, lower half of each MG cowl bulge. A large portion of Dark Green has worn off the fuselage breech cover (immediately in front of the cockpit), revealing the RLM 76 Light Blue undercoat (see color photo section, pages 33 through 48).

The Color Table on the following two pages describes the fuselage colors and their characteristics:

Colors used on the Fuselage of W.Nr. 163824		
RLM Color	**FS Equivalent**	**Comments**
Mixed Green-Gray	Between FS 34583 and FS 34672 Similar to FS 34583 but slightly lighter; similar to FS 34672 but slightly more "murky"	This pale Green-Gray color is applied to most of the fuselage sides and lower surfaces. The impression of the color is very similar to a light shade of RAF "Sky Type S". The color has been thinly applied by spray gun, and has run in several places on the starboard side. A sharp, ragged masking line divides this color from the Yellow/Green color applied to the rear fuselage on the starboard side aft of fuselage station 4. The color is a very close match for the color chip labeled "Sky" in the back of *British Aviation Colors of World War Two* (see References), and similar to the "Sky" sample in the *Ministry of Small Aircraft RAF Camouflage Color Chart* (see References), but lighter in shade. This color is similar to the paint chip described as "Green-Blue" on page 41 of *The Official Monogram Guide to German Aircraft 1935-1945* (see References), but slightly less Green. It is similar to the color labeled *Blaugrün* in Eagle Editions' *Luftwaffe Color Chart*, but slightly lighter and more Green.
RLM 76 Light Blue	Slightly darker than FS 35622	This is a lighter and more vivid Blue applied to the lower engine cowl and the lower portions of the rear portion of both starboard cowl bulges. Also used as light mottle on the cowl. Patches of RLM 76 show through the thinly-applied Green-Gray color. This color also is a close match for the RLM 76 Light Blue color chip in Model Art's *Special* on the Fw 190 D and Ta 152 (see References), but slightly lighter. The RLM 76 Light Blue shade on the aircraft is noticeably lighter and brighter than the various RLM 76 Light Blue color chips in *The Official Monogram Guide to German Aircraft 1935-1945.* However, the color chip on page 69 labeled "Light Blue (variation)" is a very close match. Interestingly, this Monogram color sample was found on another remanufactured aircraft—a Focke Wulf Fw 190 F-8/R1. The color is slightly lighter than the RLM 76 color chip in Eagle Editions' *Luftwaffe Color Chart.*

COLORS USED ON THE FUSELAGE OF W.Nr. 163824		
RLM Color	**FS Equivalent**	**Comments**
Yellow-Green	Similar to FS 34554, but slightly darker and very slightly more Yellow	Probably one of the colors sometimes incorrectly referred to as RLM 84. This color is applied only to the rear starboard fuselage aft of a sharply masked, ragged line near fuselage station 4. Similar to the color chip in the Model Art *Special* on the Fw 190 D and Ta 152 (see References), but less Green and less vivid. Almost a perfect match for the color described as "Green-Blue" on page 41 of the Monogram book.
RLM 81 **Brown-Violet**	Between FS 30118 and FS 34088 Slightly darker and less Brown than FS 30118, and slightly less Green than FS 34088	This is a distinctly Brown tone, and the lighter of the two upper-surface camouflage colors. This color has been applied thinly, especially along the top-rear of the fuselage spine. RLM 76 and/or Mixed Yellow/Gray shows through in places. Very soft, spotty but spasmodic mottle on the fuselage sides. Close match for the color chip in the Model Art *Special* on the Fw 190 D and Ta 152 (see References). Very close match for the color chip labeled "81 Brown-Violet" at the bottom left corner of page 35 in the Monogram book. The paint is somewhat lighter than the RLM 81 color sample in Eagle Editions' *Luftwaffe Color Chart.*
RLM 83 **Dark Green**	Similar in shade to FS 34083, but slightly less Green	Very Dark Green. The darker of the two upper surface camouflage colors. Very heavy application—no base color showing through here! Well spaced, but heavy, mottled spots of this color on the fuselage sides. Almost a perfect match for the color chip in the Model Art *Special* on the Fw 190 D and Ta 152 (see References). Very close match for the color chip labeled "82 Dark Green" on page 49 of the Monogram book. Slightly more Green/less Brown than the RLM 83 color sample in Eagle Editions' *Luftwaffe Color Chart.*
Primer Red	Darker than FS 31310	Red color with an Orange tint. Similar to the RLM 45 *Rotbraun* color sample in Eagle Editions' *Luftwaffe Color Chart.*

Spinner and Propeller Assembly

The spinner displays a hard-edged demarcation between its two-thirds Green and one-third White. It was common to see spinners finished in either RLM 70 Black-Green or RLM 22 Black; however, this Green appears lighter. Color comparison with paint chip sample shows that this color is a good match for RLM 71 Dark Green. The White paint has worn in some areas, exposing the Green color underneath. Over the top of these divided colors is a broad White spiral.

The spiral has been crudely brush-painted, with brush marks very evident. The White spiral is quite visible over the White one-third of the spinner. This rough spiral is visible in a photo taken just after

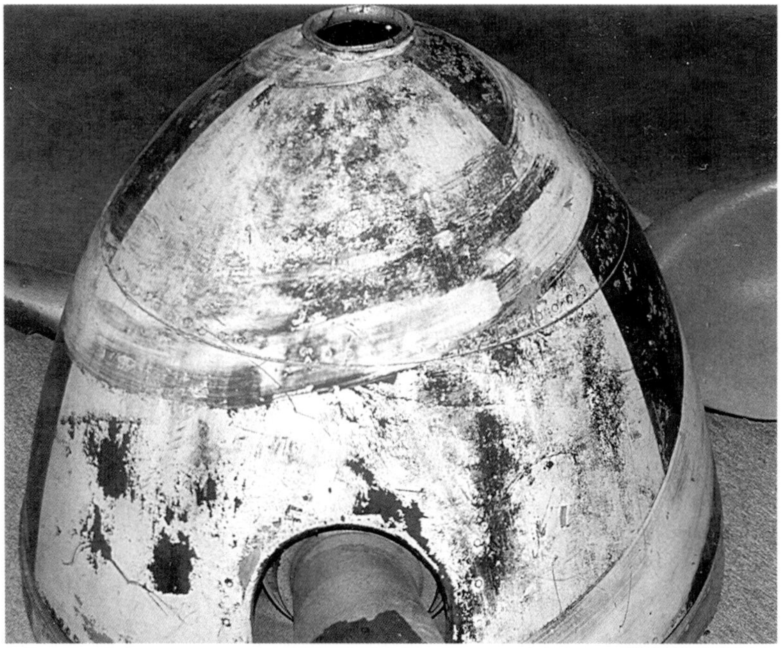

The spinner displays a hard-edged demarcation between its two-thirds Green and one-third White. It was common to see spinners finished in either RLM 70 Black-Green or RLM 22 Black; however, this Green appears lighter.

the aircraft was captured, so probably it is original.

Red primer is revealed underneath the White spiral near the tip of the spinner. The backplate of the spinner remains in natural metal. The manufacturer's code on the spinner ID plate is "fak." This indicates that the spinner was built by Oskar Epperleing, a manufacturer of vehicle accessories based in Magdeburg-Neustadt.

Propeller blades are RLM 70 Black-Green.

Wings

Several color photographs allow us to draw some conclusions about the camouflage finish of the wings (see color photos, pages 46 and 47).

The wings have the small, early-style bulge for the narrow wheels. Upper surface colors are RLM 75 Gray-Violet and RLM 83 Dark Green. The colors are divided in a non-standard pattern, with a soft edged "saw-tooth" demarcation in places. The RLM 75 appears to be a fresh coat over an existing finish. The starboard aileron has been lightly over-sprayed with color 75, with the evidence of repair clearly visible under the thin coat of Gray.

The lower surfaces of the starboard wing are painted RLM 76 Light-Blue, as is the center lower panel between the wings.

The lower surface of the port wing is painted in the mixed Green-Gray color. The aileron has received a very thin coat of the mixed Green-Gray color. RLM 76 Light Blue can be clearly seen in large patches on the aileron. The Silver on the wing, the mass-balance, and the flap is the residue of a protective skin applied during the failed export attempt around 1979.

Both wheel wells appear to be painted either RLM 02 Gray or the mixed Green-Gray—somewhat unusual in late-war Bf 109s. The top of the port-side wheel well is painted RLM 76 Light Blue (see color photo, page 46).

Tailplane

The horizontal tailplane and elevators are painted in the same upper surface colors as the wings, but without the saw-tooth edges. A small patch of Red pinking is present on top of the starboard elevator.

The lower surface of the horizontal tailplane on both sides is painted the mixed Green-Gray color of the fuselage. A narrow, rectangular patch of Red primer runs three-quarters the width of the port tailplane at the point of the elbow corner.

Both elevators appear to be painted RLM 76 Light Blue.

The rudder has spots of RLM 81 Brown-Violet over a base coat of Light Blue. The reference photos show that this Blue is considerably darker than the RLM 76 Light Blue on the bottom of the elevators. There are at least three possible explanations for this:

- the color may be mixed;
- the color may be old stocks of RLM 65;
- the color may be RLM 76 thinly sprayed over a solid coat of RLM 81 Brown-Violet (not vice-versa).

The RLM 81 spots have small diagonal streaks of RLM 83 Dark Green painted over them. These streaks appear to be sprayed, and do not intrude much onto the RLM 76 portions of the rudder. There is a rectangular patch with rounded edges in Primer Red on the lower part of the port side.

The short vertical tail has a heavy dark mottle on the port side, but seems to have been largely oversprayed with either the mixed Green/Gray or the above-mentioned mystery Blue color on the starboard side.

Undercarriage

Undercarriage gear was available for inspection. The undercarriage legs and insides of the main gear doors are RLM 76 Light Blue. A number of labels and information plates are present on the main gear legs. The wheel hubs are a light color, although it would have been unusual for paint such as RLM 76 or RLM 02 to be used. It is more likely that the usual glossy Black paint has worn off, to reveal a discolored alloy underneath. The outside of the main gear doors are sprayed with a thin coat of the mixed Green/Gray over RLM 76 Light Blue.

The tailwheel strut and scissor are painted RLM 02 Gray, as is the tailwheel bay (and entire airframe interior except for the RLM 66 Dark Gray cockpit).

Markings

The fuselage *Balkenkreuzen* are White filled with RLM 83 Dark Green in the center. The port side cross seems to have been applied over the top of the new markings, and even has overpainted new fuselage station number stencils. The dark camouflage colors show through slightly. The RLM 83 Dark Green fill has been sprayed, and has a soft-edged overspray at the bottom and on the right-hand side of the cross.

The starboard side cross has been painted before the new camouflage colors, as evidenced by a gap between the cross and the new camouflage col-

This rudder, found at Lippstadt, displays the exact characteristics of the one belonging to W.Nr. 163824 as described in the text.

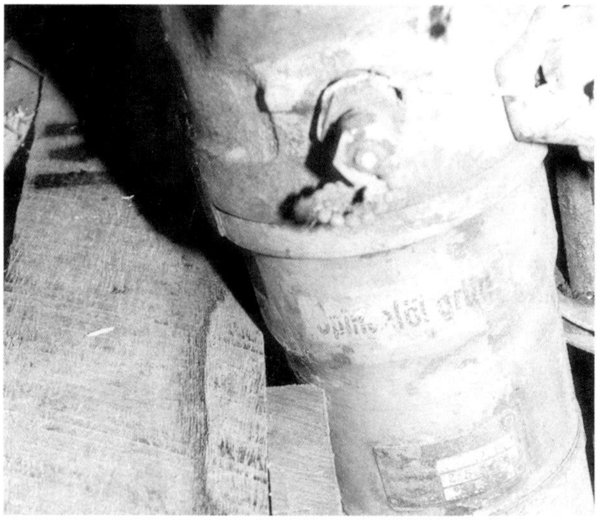

The outsides of the main gear doors are sprayed with a thin coat of the mixed Green/Gray over RLM 76 Light Blue.The tailwheel strut and scissor are painted RLM 02 Gray, as is the tailwheel bay (and the entire airframe interior except for the RLM 66 Dark Gray cockpit).

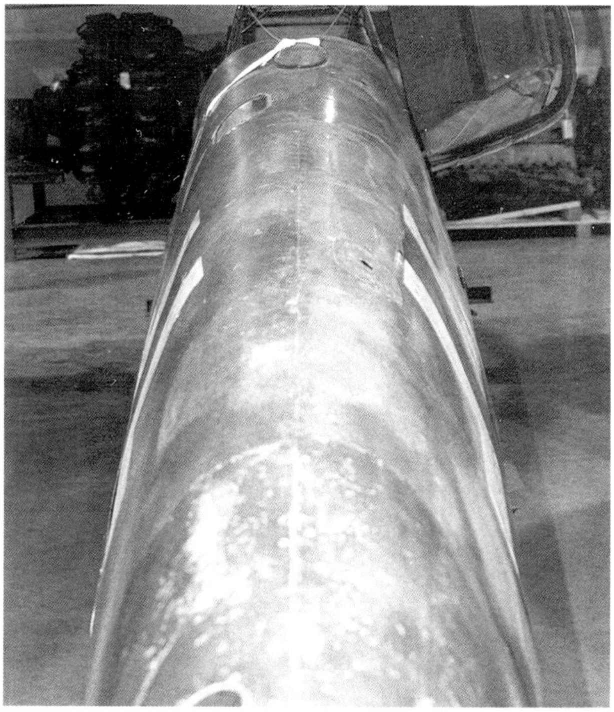

Dorsal view of Bf 109G-6 W.Nr. 163824, looking forward.

ors between which can be seen either the old color or the base coat. The Dark Green center has been masked, but applied by brush. This cross has been extensively chipped, and shows bare metal beneath.

The *Hakenkreuzen* (*swastikas*) are the mid-war Black and White style. Upper wing crosses are White skeleton outlines.

The *werknummer* is present only on the port side of the tail. It is just above the horizontal tail and overwrites the bottom of the *swastika* in tall digits. The *werknummer* on the starboard side was probably sprayed over when the new paint was applied.

No tactical markings were applied to this aircraft. Even maintenance stenciling is minimal. Footholds, panel numbers, and octane ratings are present, but hand-painted markings have replaced some stencils, including the oil-filler specifications.

The rebuild manufacturer's code and date are applied in Yellow paint under the port side of the cockpit.

Details of port side camouflage pattern.

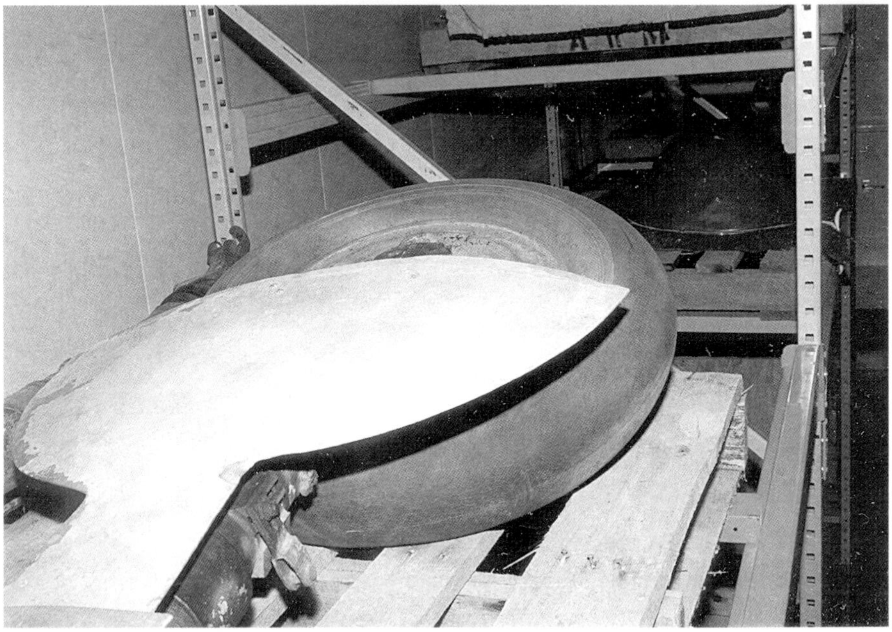

Starboard wheel (above) and port main gear door (below). The Black paint originally applied on the alloy wheel has mostly disappeared, but the mixed Green-Gray paint on the gear door remains in good condition.

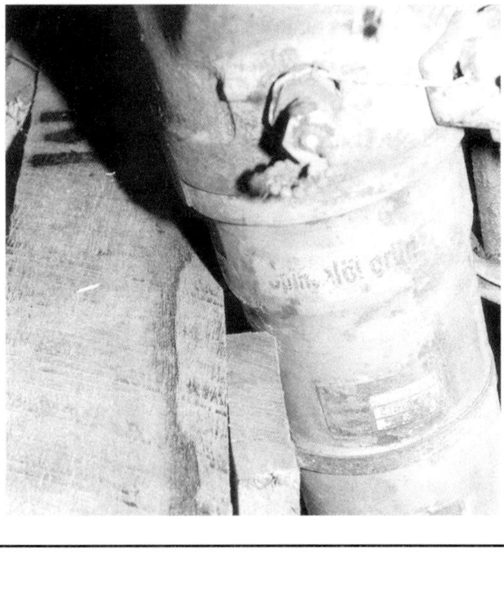

The main gear leg is painted RLM 76 Light Blue.

The Streamlined Nose – A Study of Bf 109 G-10, W.Nr. 610937

Messerschmitt Bf 109 G-10, *werknummer* 610937, was rebuilt from a Bf 109 G-14. This *werknummer* is consistent with a Bf 109 G-10 equipped with a DB605DC engine.

The Captain Michael King Smith-Evergreen Education Center in Oregon (USA) commissioned the restoration of this interesting aircraft.

The various styles of late-war Bf 109 "conformal" engine cowlings and fuselage fairings have been described in detail by M. Jean-Claude Mermet in his self-published book, *Les Messerschmitt Bf 109G-1 a K-4—Moteurs et Amenagements*, and also in Issue Number 13 of *Luftwaffe Verband* (January 1998). Mermet describes a number of structural features that identify the cowl either as Type 090, Type 100, or Type 110. The latter type of cowl has a wide, shallow oil cooler intake, a flatter bottom cowl with no "cheek blisters," and a rectangular fairing (replacing the curved style) on the port side fuselage under the windscreen. It should also be noted that there are some variations within these designations.

The forward fuselage of the restored aircraft is consistent with most of the features of a Type 100 engine cowling. The style of gun troughs, the panel lines, position of operational filler hatches, the deep oil cooler, and the lower forward cheek bulges all confirm this identity. However, there are a few mysterious omissions mentioned in the pictorial. Although it seems that there is almost no such thing as a "standard" Bf 109 G-10, this is quite close.

We are therefore provided with a unique opportunity to see the true profile of the somewhat elusive "asymmetrical cowl bulge." The following ten photographs illustrate the asymmetrical, subtle, and complex nature of the late Bf 109 engine cowl.

Firewall

Looking like a science fiction robot, this shot of a BF 109 G-10 firewall provides a good idea of the different-shaped bulges on the port and starboard sides. Note the Light Blue attachments to the side of the upper firewall. These are the internal covers for the fuselage fairings behind the cowl bulges. See how the starboard profile (left side of photo) is much flatter than the port side, which is both wider and curved outward. This complex curve extends further out as it travels forward on the engine cowl.

Port Side Cowl

The port side cowl exhibits all the features expected in a Type 090 or Type 100 cowling: namely the shorter, pressed insert and the forward vertical panel line. The curve of the bulge also is clearly illustrated at the back edge of the cowl. The continuation of the bulge to a position somewhere forward of the super-charger intake hole (then tapering off until the vertical panel line) also can be made out with the help of the reflections on the shiny metal and the backward angle of the hole itself. Note the cowl halves are slightly splayed.

Starboard Side Cowl

The starboard cowl looks closest to a Type 100. The access hatch to the cold weather starter is in the higher position. On a Type 100 cowl the old access hatch should be present immediately below the new. Usually it was welded shut; however, there is no evidence of a lower access hatch on this example. Clearly the starboard side cowl is not nearly as curved or complex as the port side. It is, in fact, quite a simple fairing with an almost flat, vertical appearance at the back of the cowl. Put simply, the sides are asymmetrical.

Port Cowl in place

The port cowl viewed from this angle demonstrates the continuation of the bulge to near the top of the cowl, behind the port machine-gun trough. This bulge covered the larger curved engine mount, itself required to clear the larger supercharger of the DB605 AS and D series engines. Also clear in this view is the deep oil cooler and the oval-shaped "bump" at the corner of the lower cowl. Note the distinct "step" at the front and rear of the oil cooler. This aircraft is an example of a Bf 109 G-10 equipped with a different style of front cowling ring without the lower position oil filler cap (normally welded shut when present on the G-10 Type 100 cowl).

Port Side Mid Fuselage

A good shot of the curved fuselage fairing typical of Type 100 cowlings. This illustrates how the fairing is simply riveted to the fuselage side. Note the small, triangular fairing similarly attached under the side of the windscreen. Once again, reflections highlight the complex angles of the port side cowling, and the extreme nature of the bulge.

Starboard Cowl—side view

Straight side view of the starboard cowling.

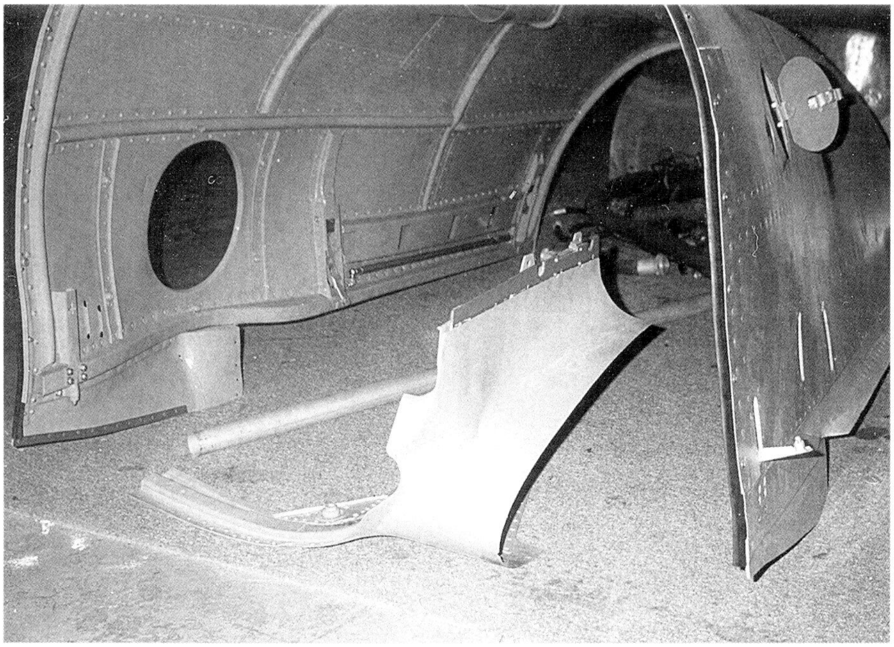

Inside of Port Cowl and Port Wingroot Panel

Note the big kink in the upper leading edge of the port wingroot panel, and the corresponding kink in the port side cowling immediately under the hole for the supercharger intake.
There is no kink on the starboard side.

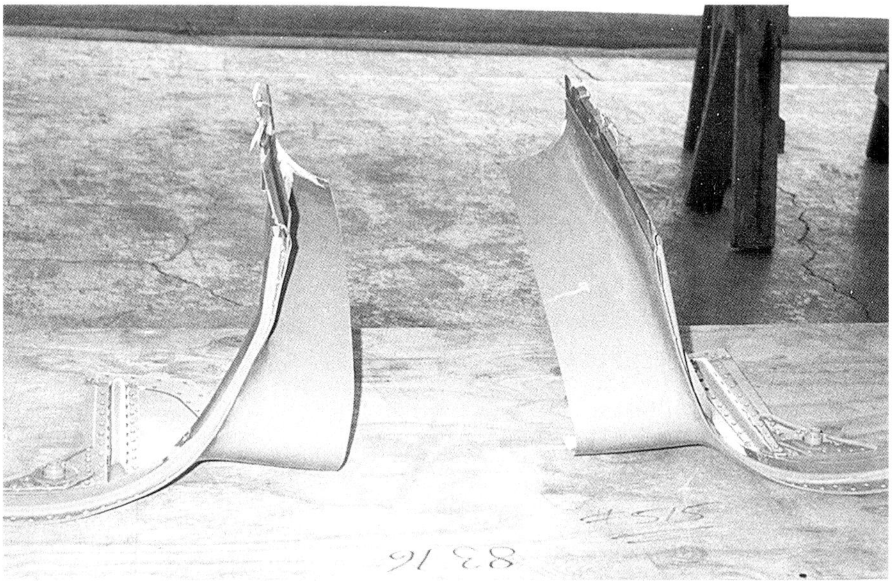

Wingroot Fairings

It is clear that the cowl intrudes significantly over the port side wingroot panel
(left side of photo).
Note the difference between the port and starboard sides when viewed at almost the same angle.

Port Side Wingroot

The wingroot panel fits right here. The front of the panel goes right under the supercharger, with the panel extending back to cover the gap between the port wing and fuselage sides. Note the temporary cover on the supercharger intake. The wing has not been installed.

Supercharger

The wing has been installed in this photograph. The big supercharger also is prominent. A portion of the curved upper engine mount can be seen at the top of the picture.

(Left) Bf 109 G-14, W.Nr. 786312 "White 14" of II./JG 53 at Braunschardt, Germany, May 1945. The spinner spiral is roughly painted by hand, and the Black RV band of JG 53 is visible under the **Gruppe** *bar on the rear fuselage. The light overspray of the* **Balkenkreuz** *is noteworthy. The aircraft is almost certainly finished in RLM 81 Brown-Violet and RLM 83 Dark Green, with an almost solid mottle on the fuselage.*

(Left) Rare photo taken at Stuttgart-Echterdingen, Germany, May 1945, of a Bf 109 K-4 "Red or Blue 8". Note the second **Gruppe** *bar and the White outlined tactical number is either Red or Blue.*

(Below, left) Despite the bulge for the compressor on the starboard cowl, this is probably a Bf 109 G-6 or G-14. This aircraft was attached to JG 53 "Pik-As" (Ace of Spades), and photographed at Braunschardt, Germany during May 1945. Note the very solid camouflage pattern from the mid-fuselage back, and the tight wavy demarcation on the leading edge of the wings between the upper and lower colors. The dark upper surface colors and low contrast suggest that this aircraft is probably finished in RLM 81 Brown-Violet and RLM 82 Dark Green. The bottom of the wings and the lower cowl are a darker shade than the lightest color on the upper engine cowling. If we assume that this lightest color is RLM 76 Light Blue, the remainder of the lower surfaces may be finished in one of the late-war "Sky" colors.

References

Luftwaffe Color Chart, profile artwork by Thomas A. Tullis. Eagle Editions Ltd., Hamilton, Montana USA, 1999. No ISBN

A very useful, fold-out color chart with actual paint samples of most RLM colors. Each sample is a generous two inches square. A description of the applications of each color also is included. Currently available from Eagle Editions Ltd., this chart features actual color chips from one of six German paint companies, Warnecke and Böhm, suppliers of aircraft paint to the Luftwaffe *during WWII.*

Kenneth A. Merrick and Thomas H. Hitchcock, *The Official Monogram Painting Guide to German Aircraft 1935-1945*. Monogram Aviation Publications, Sturbridge, Massachusetts USA, 1980. ISBN 0-914144-29-4

An excellent reference for Luftwaffe *camouflage and markings. Includes color chips. The content and format of this book revolutionized the way researchers and modelers looked at late-war German camouflage. Lamentably, it is long out of print.*

J.R. Smith, G.G. Pentland, and R.P. Lutz, *The Modeler's Luftwaffe Painting Guide*. Kookaburra Technical Publications Pty. Ltd., Melbourne, Australia, 1979. ISBN 0 85880 033 0

A companion piece to the Luftwaffe Camouflage and Markings *trilogy from Kookaburra. The color photos of the subject aircraft (and others) are invaluable. Six photos of various parts of the subject aircraft appear on page 54. One good color view of the port side of the aircraft is on page 71.*

J.R. Smith and J.D. Gallaspay, *Luftwaffe Camouflage and Markings 1935-45 Vol. 3*. Kookaburra Technical Publications Pty. Ltd., Melbourne, Australia, 1977. ISBN 0 85880 020 9

Color photographs of the subject aircraft appear in the above book on pages 92 and 132. Invaluable reference, but long out of print!

Phil Butler, *War Prizes*. Midland Counties Publications, Leicester, England, 1994. ISBN 0 904597 86 5

A photograph of the subject aircraft W. Nr. 163824 appears on page 151.

Carl Hildebrandt, *Broken Eagles 2—Bf 109 G/K, Part 1*. Fighter Pictorials, Perkiomenville, PA, 1988. No ISBN

——, *Broken Eagles 3—Bf 109 G/K, Part 2*, Fighter Pictorials, Perkiomenville, PA, 1988. No ISBN

Two excellent pictorial studies of captured, abandoned, and wrecked Messerschmitt Bf 109s found by the Allies in their march across Western Europe at war's end.

Model Art Messerschmitt Bf 109 G/K Augsburg Eagle. Model Art Co. Ltd., Tokyo, Japan, No. 290. No ISBN

Focke-Wulf Fw 190 D & Ta 152, Model Art Special No. 8. Model Art Co. Ltd., Tokyo, Japan, 1989 (reprinted 1997). No ISBN

Color chips on page 135 of the above publication as referred to in text. These samples were quite close to colors found on the subject aircraft.

However, BEWARE—there is massive variation between the samples claimed to be the same color in other Model Art Specials. As far as I know, these samples may vary even in the same publication. Cross-reference against the FS numbers listed above to be sure.

David H. Klaus, *IPMS Color Cross-Reference Guide*. Published by the author, San Bernardino, CA, 1991 (sixth reprinting). No ISBN

A great starting point for color research. This publication includes an FS595B color fan.

Jochen Prien & Peter Rodeike, *Messerschmitt Bf 109 F, G & K Series—an Illustrated Study*. Schiffer Military Histories, Atglen, Pennsylvania USA, 1993. ISBN 0-88740-424-3

Well laid-out and chronological history of mid- to late Bf 109s. Lots of pictures, and the best way to identify DB605D and DB605AS variants—an excellent summary of conformal bulge variations.

Shigeru Nohara and Masatsugu Shiwaku, *Aero Detail No. 5 Messerschmitt Bf 109 G*. Dai Nippon Kaiga Co. Ltd., Tokyo, Japan, 1992. ISBN 4-499-20589-1

Camouflage Color Chart for RAF Day Fighters (WWII—Northern Europe) UK-1-1. Ministry of Small Aircraft Production, Quebec, Canada, no date. No ISBN

John Tanner (editor), *British Aviation Colors of World War Two*. Arms and Armour Press, London, England, 1986. ISBN 0-85368-271-2

An excellent one-stop description of all major British Air Ministry orders from April 1939 to October 1944. Includes color chips for all standard RAF colors.

Jerry Crandall, *Doras of the Galland Circus*. Eagle Editions Ltd., Hamilton, Montana USA, 1999. ISBN 0-9660706-2-3; LCC Number 99-94772

David E. Brown and David Wadman, *History, Camouflage and Markings of JV 44, JG 6, and JG 1 Focke Wulf 190 Ds. Experten Decals No. 3*. Experten Historical Aviation Research Inc., Calgary, Canada, 1995. No ISBN.

David E. Brown, *Luftwaffe RLM Colors 81, 82 & 83—A Commentary on their Evolution and Usage, Parts 1, 2, and 3*. Experten Historical Aviation Research Inc., Bedford, Canada, 1997. (Published on the Internet in rec.models.scale newsgroup). No ISBN.

Jean-Claude Mermet, *Les Messerschmitt Bf 109 G-1 à K-4—Moteurs et aménagements* (2e Édition). Published by the author, Aix-En-Provence, France, 1995. No ISBN

——, "The Messerschmitt Bf 109 G-10." Article in the periodical *Luftwaffe Verband Journal*, Issue 13, January 1998.

The Author

Born in 1960, Australian author Brett Green can trace his long-time fascination with aviation history to childhood.

Beginning with enthusiastic model aircraft building, and later membership as a cadet in the Air Training Corps, Royal Australian Air Force (RAAF), his interests in aviation research, photography, and scale model building have grown considerably with the passage of time.

Brett has written numerous review, research, and modeling articles for aviation publications including *IPMS News And Views* and *Australian Models and Hobbies*, and several of his pieces have been translated for publication in foreign-language magazines. *Augsburg's Last Eagles* is his first full-length aviation writing effort.

In March of 1998 he launched the internet-based "webzine" *HyperScale* (<http://www.hyperscale.com>), which has proved popular not only for its articles on aviation history, but for its lively interactive discussion groups, as well.

Today Brett lives with his wife, Debra, and children Charlotte and Sebastian in Sydney, where he has pursued a career in the telecommunications industry for over two decades.

We welcome Brett Green to Eagle Editions Ltd.

Also available in the

Library of Eagles

EagleFiles #1

Doras of the Galland Circus

History of the "long-nose" Fw 190 D-9s flying cover for Me 262 jets of the *Luftwaffe*'s famed "Galland Circus." 72 pages; ten color pages, 8½" x 11" color softcover.

US$28.00

Green Hearts: First in Combat with the Dora 9

Fabulous pictorial essay of Fw 190 D-9 "Doras" flying dangerous defense of the Reich missions in the closing days of World War II. 351 pages; 4 color pages plus 10 double-page color aircraft profile gatefolds, 8½" x 11" hardcover with full-color dustjacket.

US$85.00

EagleFiles #2

"Yellow 10"

Story of the last Fw 190 D-13, restored to flying condition, plus the story of Bf 109 G-10/U4 "Black 2"; their near-loss and restorations. 88 pages; 14 color pages, 8½" x 11" color softcover.

US$30.00

Eagles Illustrated #1

Fighters of World War II

Over fifty full-color aircraft profiles, plus color notes and technical data on Allied and *Luftwaffe* aircraft from World War II. Horizontal format, 11" x 8½" color softcover.

US$18.95

Eagles Illustrated #2

Allies in the Pacific

Over fifty full-color aircraft profiles, plus color notes and technical data on Allied aircraft in the Pacific during World War II. Horizontal format, 11" x 8½" color softcover.

US$18.95

For these and other aviation history-related items, visit our website at **www.eagle-editions.com**.
Call or write for our catalog, or for more information:
Eagle Editions, Ltd., P.O. Box 580, Hamilton, MT 59840 USA • (406) 363-5415 • Fax (406) 375-9270

"White 8"

A Messerschmitt Bf 109 K-4, possibly from I./JG 52, photographed in May 1945. This aircraft crash-landed behind American lines. The camouflage finish is RLM 81 Brown-Violet and RLM 83 Dark Green, with a dense mottle on the fuselage sides. The fuselage cross is filled in with RLM 83 Dark Green. Lower surfaces are finished in a dirty shade of RLM 76 Light Blue. The upper wing has an unusual White stripe over the wing-tip panel line. The spinner is painted Black with a White spiral.

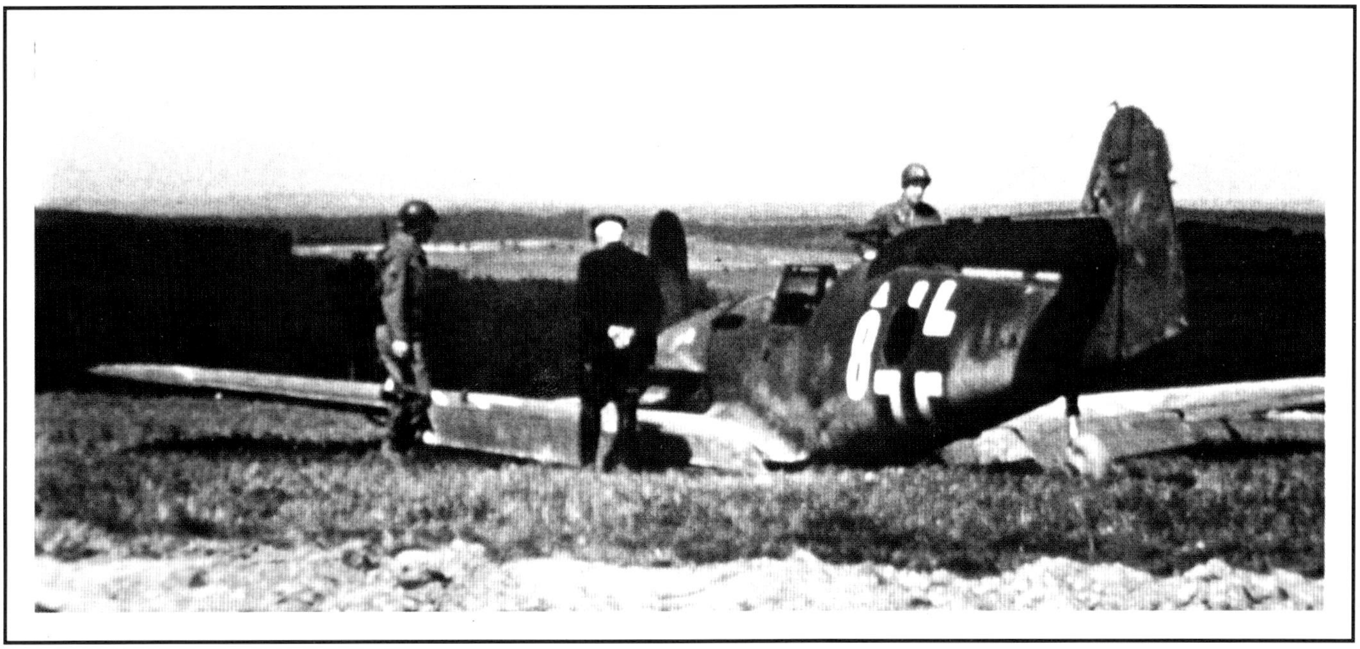

A Messerschmitt Bf 109 G-10, "White 3", possibly from I./JG 52 in May 1945. This aircraft crash-landed behind American lines. It features large wheel bulges and wide tires, but retains the short tailwheel strut. The camouflage finish is 74/75 Grays, with a dense mottle on the fuselage sides. The fuselage cross is filled in with RLM 74 Dark Gray. The upper wing has an unusual White stripe over the wing-tip panel line.

An unidentified Bf 109 G-6 or G-14 behind US lines in Germany. This aircraft features small wheel bulges on the upper wing and the clear vision **Erla Haube** *canopy. Camouflage appears to be RLM 74 Gray-Green and RLM 75 Gray-Violet with patches of RLM 81 Brown-Violet and a very dark color, possibly RLM 70 Black-Green. The spinner is Black with a White spiral. The light-colored patch on the leading edge of the wing may repeat the aircraft number, "Black 16".*

$30.00 USD

ISBN 0-9660706-5-8

53000>

9 780966 070651